Not All Black Girls Know How to Eat

A Story of **Bulimia**

Stephanie Covington Armstrong

Lawrence Hill Books

Library of Congress Cataloging-in-Publication Data

Covington Armstrong, Stephanie.
    Not all Black girls know how to eat : a story of bulimia / Stephanie
Covington Armstrong.
        p. cm.
    ISBN 978-1-55652-786-9 (pbk.)
    1. Covington Armstrong, Stephanie—Health.
    2. Covington Armstrong, Stephanie—Mental health.
    3. Covington Armstrong, Stephanie—Childhood and youth.
    4. Bulimia—United States—Case studies.   5. Bulimia—
Patients—United States—Biography.   6. African American
women—Biography.   7. African American women—Mental
health—Case studies.   8. African American families—New York
(State)—New York.   9. Bedford-Stuyvesant (New York, N.Y.)—
Biography.   10. New York (N.Y.)—Biography.
    I. Title.

RC552.B84C68 2009
616.85′2630092--dc22
    [B]   2009007354

Cover design: TG Design
Front cover photos: Stephanie Covington Armstrong as a young girl
    courtesy of the author; lower photo by Thomas Northcut/
    Photodisc/ Getty Images
Back cover photo: courtesy of Roger Ericksen
Interior design: Pamela Juárez

Published by Lawrence Hill Books
An imprint of Chicago Review Press, Incorporated
814 North Franklin Street
Chicago, Illinois 60610
ISBN 978-1-55652-786-9
Printed in the United States of America
5 4 3 2 1

To Zoë, who taught me how to be a mother;
and to my sisters, Cecilia, who couldn't bear the pain
of childhood and chose a lifetime of addiction instead,
and Renee, who has always loved me unconditionally;
and to my mother, who grew up right alongside us.

Contents

A Note from the Author

This is my story. It is not a how-to book on recovery or a love letter to any one program or practice. This is simply the truth about my journey and what worked for me as I navigated the road from food addiction to recovery. I know of many hospital programs and inpatient recovery programs that work miracles, but I did not have the financial means or the health insurance to be able to afford those. Nor would I have trusted specialists to help me. But that has more to do with where I come from than with their abilities. For a long time, allowing myself to become dependent on therapists and other professionals was foreign to me and, even worse, shameful. I had to grow up and learn to leave behind my ignorant beliefs that as a black woman I needed to suffer in silence, that somehow my legacy of strong, independent ancestors did not allow me to lean on anyone outside my community. These beliefs swallowed me up and separated me from the very people who would have been able to help me. But that was something I learned along the way.

I am an addict; my drug of choice was food. This book is for people who have suffered themselves or who know someone suffering. And for those who wake up every Monday morning ready to start a new miracle diet and yet do not know that their lives are controlled by their relationship to food. There are so many forms of eating disorders and disordered eating on the spectrum, and unfortunately many people are unaware of how deeply these disorders can affect their lives.

My problems with food disintegrated into full-blown, textbook eating disorders, and they had nothing to do with vanity. Bulimia and anorexia are painful states of isolation and depression; they are not quick ways to stay skinny. These are not diseases that I could live with while maintaining sanity.

Everybody deserves a chance to live an addiction-free life. For me, as for others, it isn't easy, nor is there a rule book to follow. If there were, I would have already broken each and every rule.

This story takes place from my birth until the age of twenty-seven. The years I spent in my addiction were the longest, most painful, and most self-loathing imaginable. But without bulimia I would have never been forced to take an inward journey, to get to know myself and heal the wounds of my childhood. For that I am grateful.

If you catch glimpses of yourself in the pages of this book or if you see similarities to someone you love, I believe it is because even though every person struggling with an eating disorder is unique, there are universal similarities in our stories. Millions of people struggle with weight and food issues, and the diet industry is a billion-dollar business fostering the message that thinness is the only way to find lasting happiness and love. That was a hidden belief of mine, one that kept me imprisoned in my addiction, striving for unattainable body perfection. I desperately needed one area of my life to control, and naively I believed food was the part that would be easy, but I was wrong. I hope that by reading this book, you will find options to give you the strength to live one more day abstinently, free of food or body obsession.

Eating . . .

Grabbing a handful of long rope braids, I pull them back so they don't swing into my face. Taking my index and middle fingers from my other hand, I shove them deep down my throat. I force hearty chunks of food, then more food, then greenish bile, to surge forward into the toilet, intent on emptying the contents of my stomach. Tapeworm-length reconstituted doughnuts come up first, then vanilla mocha swirl ice cream–covered cereal. The popcorn I just ate heaves forward followed by the majority of two peanut butter and jelly sandwiches, but they don't reemerge in their entirety, and I begin to panic. My heart races. I am anxious; fear consumes me. Like a zombie, I march into the kitchen, hurriedly scoop more ice cream into a bowl, then shovel it in my mouth, coating my throat for the abuse ahead. I retrieve the residual box of doughnuts tossed into the bottom of the garbage, covered with newspapers, empty juice boxes, and old food. I had stuffed them deep into the garbage to deter myself from another binge. Clearly, it didn't work.

Polishing off the ice cream and doughnuts, I search the fridge, a desperate scavenger, seeking other sweet, purge-friendly options. Sometimes my binges are all sweet, some-times they are salty, and other times they are mixed.

Finding the frozen pancakes I made a week earlier, I fling them into the microwave, impatiently banging the timer button. I grab the hot pancakes, slather them with jelly, and singe my tongue as I gobble them down. But it doesn't matter, because I barely taste them.

This is not about pleasure. It is all about pain.

Exhausted from chewing, I want to be done until I remember the French bread I bought the day before. I feel it beckoning me. I cut a hunk of butter and place it in a ramekin along with a grated clove of garlic and toss the mixture into the microwave. When the timer goes off, I remove the butter, pour it on the French bread, and chew through my fatigue. My jaw aches.

Stuffed to the gills I return to the scene of the crime. This time I remember to pull my braids into a ponytail, gathering them with an elastic band. My two fingers, still reeking of the binge twenty minutes earlier, are thrust to the back of my throat, forcing the slightly digested food to propel forward into the toilet. I repeat this ritual several times, then as if I were in a trance I rise and cup a handful of water from the sink into my mouth and swallow.

I return to the toilet and try to throw up one last time, and I am rewarded when all that comes out is a thin layer of greenish mucus. Pleased that all the food I'd binged on is now swirling down the drain, I grab some toilet paper, soak it with water, and clean around the bowl and the floor and walls. I always cover my tracks in case company comes over, especially a man. Rising, I wash my hands, brush my teeth, and clean the splashed water from the sink.

A dizzy spell causes me to grip the sides of the sink. In the mirror I stare at the chocolate brown. It is me, only different. My eyes are bloodshot and watering, my normally high cheek-bones are puffy, deep lines are etched into bags under my eyes, and I look a mess.

Who is this? I wonder. *Why have I become this? Where is the self-control I was taught from birth?*

But there is no getting around this truth; I am still the same little black girl who grew up in the Bedford-Stuyvesant section of Brooklyn, living far below the poverty line. And I am still sad, lonely, and afraid. How in God's name have I gotten here? And why?

For years, I wrestled with writing this book, losing my anonymity, revealing my shame. I even went so far as to write the first hundred pages, but they read hollow, as if Disney had sanitized the experience and turned the horror into an acceptable fairy tale. I knew I could only access the truth if I let go of what people might say or think. *Next week, next month, next year*, I promised whenever I opened my laptop. But it was never now, never today.

I often wondered, *Will I ever be ready, can I grow brave enough to expose my deep-seated self-loathing? To tell strangers I willingly stuck my face where others put their asses? With a little more self-discovery, a lot more recovery, will I be able to set forth on the inward journey into the unhappiest period of my life?*

I told myself it is normal to shove your past under a rug, never to be seen or heard from again, but as hard as I tried, I could not do that. I could not forget. Nonetheless, I was afraid to explore that past, fearing that writing about my experience, my dark night of the soul, might invite it in again. My addiction had swallowed me whole, consumed me in a tidal wave of raw, unfulfilled expectations, betrayal, rage, and a never-ending sadness.

Only I knew the self-destruction I had lived through. Instead of being in the world, I survived in the underbelly, a black hole of depression and fear, and yet no one ever noticed. I became a master of disguising my addiction. And even though I read every popular self-help book, took numerous self-aware-ness, love-yourself workshops, practiced yoga, and meditated, I still knew very little about something as ordinary as eating. I had taken food—the very thing that sustains life—and used it as a weapon, nearly killing myself. Food became my drug, and I wholeheartedly committed myself to the addiction. Shouldn't I leave it all in the past, along with my bulimia?

My relapse came suddenly and without warning. In the throes of pain and desperation, I retreated to my unhealthiest cop-ing mechanism, bingeing and purging. It was a hell as famil-iar as it was brutal. Abandoning fifteen years of abstinence, everything about this time was different. I was no longer the naive girl shoving her fingers down her throat believing I did it just to lose those last ten pounds. I knew exactly what I was doing, and I was aware of the consequences. I wanted control, even though I knew it didn't work, and yet I was too pained to stop myself. Bulimia was my way of dying, slowly, brutally, and surely. My daily actions became my unspoken suicide pact with myself, intended to obliterate the parts of me I had come to hate. If the rest of me got killed in the crossfire, oh well. Who cared, anyway? I had hurt people in the name of love, and I didn't deserve this life of abstinence, peace, and security I had created. Unlike before, I had no intention of seeking recovery from this addiction, of twelve-stepping my way to a new free-dom and a new happiness. I did not believe I deserved to be happy. In this, my time of need, my crisis, bulimia rescued me from an avalanche of pain and burned feelings, but most of all from the shame and self-loathing that threatened to consume me. I hated sliding my fingers down my throat, searching for the relief I could not find staring back at myself in the mirror. And as much as I tried to quash my feelings with every bite, they all came rushing in between binges.

I knew this could not go on forever. My relapse propelled me backward to the place where it all began, and I knew a deeper healing would have to start. There was still so much work to do. If I was going to get to the other side of this, to survive my own shame, I would finally have to relive my life word by word, to remove the rose-colored glasses, discard my torn, dirty running shoes, and stand still. I would have to take complete ownership of every choice that had brought me back into this hell. A blind person could see that I had nowhere to run, because wherever I went, there I was—an incredible mess.

And so, after two weeks of throwing up morning, noon, and night, I did the thing I needed to do to restore myself to the living: I stepped back in my memory to the complex life that guaranteed I would end up with some kind of addiction. I had chosen food over drugs, alcohol, men, gambling, codependency, or any of the isms. Like a good little addict, over the years I had told so many versions of my life story in order to elicit the response I needed at the moment: love, forgiveness, pity, financial support, guilt, and so on. I had been too diseased to recognize that the person I had hurt the most with these lies was me. It kept me from taking responsibility for the life that I had chosen to live, and it stopped me from being whole and complete. It was not the way I wanted to live anymore. Now it was, simply, time to tell the truth.

Part One

Before

A Hungry Childhood

I grew up in the Bed-Stuy section of Brooklyn, the youngest of three girls with an unwed mother barely out of her teens. My earliest memories are either too vague or those repeated to me by my older sisters. I have no memory of my own before the age of six.

At age twenty-two, my mother had three girls, ages five and under, and no help from our three absentee fathers. The weight of her parental responsibility crushed her youth and threatened to destroy her future.

One dreary autumn morning, we rode a crowded subway train to downtown Brooklyn, only our mother aware of our destination. Based on the early hour, coupled with my mother's somber expression, we assumed we were headed to the welfare office. My mother worked full-time but still needed food stamps in order to feed us. Because she had a job and paid taxes, she needed to have a second social security number without a job attached in order to collect benefits. On her meager income, even food was a luxury, and that's where the government's help came in handy. In order to qualify for aid you had to be living well below the poverty line, which we were, but to Uncle Sam we were simply straddling the fence. Four people should have been able to survive on twelve thousand dollars a year . . . before taxes. The welfare office was not a place for kids to be kids; the swelling roomful of children took on their parents' anxieties, externalizing their worry and stress by bouncing off the gray walls and behaving like caged animals.

But it wasn't the welfare office we entered. We four arrived at a large dingy office of a Catholic organization. While the nuns watched, arms crossed under their breasts, our mother knelt in front of us three and explained.

"I have to put you in foster care because I cannot take care of you," she said. "This will not be for long. I promise to bring you all home soon."

Our mother then agonizingly handed us over to a nondescript nun, a woman with a practiced compassion who had really seen too much to have an authentic emotional connection to another mother relinquishing her children that day. Knowing my mother and her avoidance of emotions, I imagine her steely body stiffened against the shame of abandoning the three girls she had no business bringing into the world in the first place. My middle sister Renee and I were sent to live with a large Puerto Rican woman—Mrs. Lucy—her son Raymond, her daughter Mariel, and her husband, while my older sister Cecilia went alone with a stern-faced woman and her husband. That was the moment we went from being a family of four females to being wards of New York State, continuing my family legacy of children separated from mothers, assigned our own personal case file numbers and social workers.

Although I can't remember the details, I can imagine how I felt being separated from my mother at almost two years old, to hunger for her touch, her smell, her sound. I believe that was the moment I began what would become a lifetime of hungering, a denial of needing anything or anyone, and a loneliness that sits in my soul and beckons me every day.

During the year that followed, my mother kept up her weekly visits to us at Mrs. Lucy's in the Bronx. She told us that Cecilia missed us, but we never saw her in the entire time of our separation. In subsequent years, as my sisters and I grew up, Renee and I were attached, but Cecilia always hovered outside of our closeness, making me wonder if this is where that break began.

My mother took us to the park, bought us candy, and reminded us that we belonged to her. She worked two jobs in order to get back on her feet and reunite us, but I was a toddler, and the Puerto Rican woman who potty trained me, rocked me to sleep, and always provided dessert after dinner was quickly replacing my memory of my mother, and she knew it. My mom is at least ten shades lighter than I am, and I'm sure to a toddler she and the Puerto Rican woman had a resemblance, allowing my memory of my mother to transfer onto Mrs. Lucy, even though my thin mother was a stick figure compared with her. But I was a baby who needed a mother, and the one in front of me had to do.

Returning Home

More than a year later my mother reestablished herself and began to collect her children. I went home first, then Cecilia, and two months later Renee followed. My mother took us to our new home, a second-floor railroad flat, where one room bled into the next absent a hallway, in the Bushwick section of Brooklyn. Our bedroom was a windowless room with bunk beds across from the lone bathroom. To one side of our bedroom was my mother's room, which was intended to be the living room, and past that room was the one we used as a living room. On the other side was the kitchen, a bright yellow room with plenty of windows, where I remember having my ears pierced, getting my hair hot combed for Easter.

But the thing that holds the most significance is dinnertime. I hated my mother's cooking, which meant that eventually I came to hate the kitchen. Because you entered our apartment through the kitchen, it was impossible to avoid. Normally, the kitchen is the centerpiece of a home, where the warmth from the oven mirrors the warmth from the mother and spreads throughout the family. This was not the case for us.

A couple of months after being reunited, my mother surprised us with a rare treat. On Renee's fifth birthday, my mother took the train to Mrs. Maxwell's Bakery on Atlantic Avenue and bought Renee their famous strawberry shortcake. Because the cake sat in the center of the table seducing me, for once I ate my dinner without issue. Finally, there was some reward. After dinner we sang "Happy Birthday," then dug into our rich, foamy cake.

As we started to eat, Renee blurted out, "I liked it at Mrs. Lucy's house better."

In that instant, the warmth in my mother's eyes chilled, then hardened, until she no longer resembled the same person she had been a moment before. My mother's pained heart contracted as her hand unfurled, and she slapped Renee across the cheek and sent her to bed before Renee could realize the sting of her words or finish her cake. My mother didn't often take chances showing us her love, and here it had been trampled on by her five-year-old.

Apparently, Renee's birthday at Mrs. Lucy's house the year before held a brighter place in her mind. According to my sister, Mrs. Lucy took great pride in preparing tasty meals, always followed by dessert, which made this birthday less of a big deal. My mother, exhausted from overwork and little pay, dumped water-drenched vegetables out of cans to be served alongside partially fried chicken, tasteless meatloaf, or overcooked beef. Food was an afterthought to my mother, a necessary bother that went along with ensuring she'd be allowed to keep her children. As a child, my mother survived by stealing milk from neighboring doorsteps in order to feed her five younger siblings, who were often left in her care. To my mother food was for survival, rarely for pleasure.

Growing up, my mother and her siblings were often dispersed to the four corners of the five boroughs to live with relatives, in foster care, in a boys' home. My mother was raised in a Catholic orphanage, while one slightly "retarded" (the word used back then) aunt languished in a state hospital for almost twenty-five years, until my determined mother rescued her from the shocking conditions and isolation and patched together her five living siblings into a makeshift family.

My grandmother, who was raised by her aunt, preferred to spend her time chasing men, racing from herself, rather than raising the children she brought into the world. My grandmother's mother died when she was three years old. From eighteen she worked as a domestic, caring for other people's—white people's—children and homes. To her, men were not a luxury item; she needed a man the way others need food or water, and she wouldn't let anyone deter her.

Years later, when my grandmother was diagnosed with Alzheimer's and began to lose her memory, many family members wondered if that was her way of ending her life in peace, without painful reminders of the children whose childhoods she abandoned. My mother never had anyone show her how to be a mother, how to show love, or how to prepare edible food.

Never having had a stable family of her own, my mother emulated the rituals of television families, imitating their dinnertime routines. Nightly, we sat down to dinner as a family and were ordered to finish everything on our plates. My sisters, who also found my mother's cooking objectionable, gobbled down the contents of their plates, desperate to get it over with, and were excused from the table as I shifted the food on my plate back and forth, over and over again. My mother gave a look that had the ability to intimidate adults, so she had no problem keeping her girls in check. But unlike my sisters, I wore down my mother's patience with a silent refusal to conform to her program.

Motherhood and my mother were strongly incompatible, like oil and water or Democrats and Republicans. Had my mother worked through her own complex parenting issues before having children of her own, she might have been less burdened by the children she did have. Renee and Cecilia had clearer recollections than I had of our family's yearlong separation and did not feel secure enough to rock the boat. As the youngest, I had no memory of being sent away; I could focus only on the disgusting food in front of me and how I did not want to eat it. Each night the dinner became our battlefield, with me refusing to eat my mother's cooking.

Never before or since those days had I or anyone else in my memory ever defied my mother. Challenging her was not something anyone ever attempted, at least not that we kids had witnessed. Her anger and retaliation shook fear into everyone's heart, including my grown uncles' and my grandmother's. My mother famously held people hostage with her temper, forcing family members to back down rather than have her anger unleashed on them.

But no number of threats could make me consume canned beets and undercooked chicken or whatever indigestible excuse for food had landed on my plate. I would sit in silence as my mother ranted about how hard she worked to provide for us —who was I to turn up my nose? She would work herself into a state at what she considered to be a huge insult. Her voice elevated octaves. She shouted memories from her own childhood of having to steal bread and milk to feed her younger siblings because her own mother would go missing for days. If my sisters were still sitting with us, one of them would glare while the other kicked me under the table. How could I give Mom a difficult time? I was too selfish, they swore. Didn't I know how hard she worked?

The only thing I knew for sure was that I was never going to eat her cooking, and no amount of yelling or guilt could force me. I deserved to eat food prepared with love, not thrown together in a fit like this was some orphanage.

Eventually my eyelids would grow heavy as my head lowered onto the dinner plate, peas getting mashed between my cornrows. My mother would pass into the kitchen and scream at me to wake up and eat before I received a beating. Usually, in other cases, the angry glint in my mother's flashing hazel eyes sent me springing into action, but somehow her threats failed to elicit the standard reaction when it came to food. I held my ground. She always seemed one fraction of a second from making good on her promise to knock me into next year, but in the next breath all her anger deflated, and she'd send me off to bed. It was as if her withdrawal was a silent confirmation about the inedible quality of her cooking.

My mother came from an environment where every scrap received in life was hard won. If she was lucky enough to have dinner, she knew not to expect seconds. In her world, you never ever complained. In the orphanage where she was raised, you ate what was put in front of you because wasting food was sinful and a punishable offense. The nuns drilled the seven deadly sins into the heads of their charges along with catechism and all things Catholic. The idea that she would take the time and effort to serve a real meal for her family and that one of her hardheaded children would refuse to eat it was more than my mother could take.

As I was sent off to bed, instead of the sense of relief that I expected, I felt saddened by my mother's withdrawal. It felt unnatural to win against her. It's not that I preferred a harsh punishment, but as her child I had come to expect consequences for my actions. And I quickly learned that my mother's intolerance of me had been adopted by her older children. My sisters pounced as soon as I entered the bedroom, calling me a stupid troublemaker, but I didn't care. It was another night on which I had done the impossible and lived to tell about it.

Even so, I knew food for us was a luxury not to be taken for granted. Once my mother paid all the rent and whatever bills she could with her meager salary, there wasn't much left over for food. There were many nights of almost-bare cupboards, butter sandwiches, and shaking roaches out of the cereal box before I could pour myself a bowl. So I felt conflicted when my mother could actually afford to feed me and I refused to eat; there were equal measures of guilt and shame mixed with my smug self-satisfaction.

If I had been one in a litter of puppies, I would have been the obvious runt of the bunch; I would always be inches shorter than the other females in my house. Our nightly fights were the only time that my mother failed to dominate me. When standing my ground, I did not feel small and insignificant. It was symbolic, and perhaps that was the moment my need for control cemented itself around food.

We changed addresses often, always a lateral move from one roach- and mouse-infested tenement to the next. As soon as my sisters and I became comfortable in a new school, making new friends, we would invariably find my mother packing our belongings, and once again we'd be off. By high school graduation my primary education included nine different institutions: four elementary schools, three junior highs, and two high schools. I became a master at fitting in quickly, disguising my insecurity with silly jokes and tall tales. I made friends easily, bonding with those from better circumstances whose cupboards and refrigerators filled to overflowing with a variety of delicious foods.

Stay-at-home mothers were my favorites; they were so unlike my own mother, who needed to work full-time during the day and attend school at night, constantly stretching for a wider landscape. These mothers were always welcoming and pleasant, as if seeing my little face perched at their table for afternoon snacks five days in a row wasn't a problem. They baked cookies, provided instruction, brought us sandwiches as we did our homework, and made me crave the calm consistency of their apartments. I'd even put up with an incompatible friend if she had a stay-at-home mom.

Luckily my mother had always insisted on respect for adults and good manners, so I was on my best behavior away from home. I feared adults telling my mother that I had smart-mouthed them or done something to suggest I lacked home training.

Just as my mother took pride in our manners, she also made sure we were put together and looked our best before we left the house. In our neighborhood people were quick to look down on a parent who let her children out into the world looking like something the cat dragged through the mud. We understood that our appearance reflected, positively or negatively, on our mother.

This wasn't nearly that important to me as the youngest. Because my mother worked, she rarely had time to give me the once-over before I went out into the world anyway. My sisters' suggestions fell on deaf ears, as I'd wear whatever mismatched outfit interested me. Of course, I always had my butt back in the house before my mother came home so that she wouldn't know I had embarrassed her with my clothing choices.

Weekends were spent with my large reconstituted family. My mother virtually erased any memories of her and her sib-lings being raised separately, forging a blind trust with them as adults. Childhood memories of time spent together were non-existent, so they might as well have been strangers. But to my mother, DNA trumped unfamiliarity, and she and her siblings picked up as if they had seen one another consistently—not ten or more years earlier. Their bond was absolute; they could not have been closer had they been raised under one rickety roof.

Most weekends my sisters, cousins, and I arrived unan-nounced at my grandmother's house with food stamps and knapsacks overflowing with clothes. The car, usually driven by my aunt Susie's boyfriend Sonny, would pull in front of my grandmother's one-story house on Herkimer Street. Reminis-cent of clowns in a car at the circus, we kids would pile out, all five or six of us, and rush to my grandmother's door. As soon as the door swung open and my grandmother was in sight, the car would speed off, refusing to slow for the possibility of random kids running into the street after stray balls. My grandmother, gray since age twenty-five, would scream after my mother and my aunt for dumping us off—me, Cecilia, Renee, Deborah, Felicia, and sometimes their younger brother Daniel—knowing full well she had an important card game to win. My grandmother worked her whole life as a domestic, but by the time I came along she was semiretired, her major source of income both illegal and legal gambling. She played bid whist and blackjack. She also played the numbers, an illegal street lottery in the hood that's been around since long before lotteries became legal. My grandmother's lifelong fear of flying abated once—long enough for her to fly to Las Vegas to gamble for the weekend.

By the time I was ten I knew how to win at too many card games for my mother's peace of mind: spades, bid whist, tonk, and others. My mother considered card games the road to future unemployment and scolded my grandmother for teaching us such filth. She worked hard to keep her three girls from becoming ghettofied. We were not allowed to use slang in front of my mother. "Get the dictionary and find that word," she'd bark whenever one of us slipped the latest colloquialism into a conversation. Nobody, especially my sisters and I, could ever accuse my mother of being fun.

My aunt Bonita, who was only seven years older than me, usually watched us for our grandmother, but she had a serious boyfriend who demanded her attention, which allowed us to run wild in the streets at all hours of the night when she was entertaining and our grandmother was working or playing cards. Sometimes we'd sit on the neighbor's steps till three in the morning, playing "yo' mama" games. Nothing equals the humidity of New York City summer nights, and since it wasn't safe to leave your doors open to catch whatever breeze there might be, we'd find ourselves outside, along with the majority of neighborhood kids. Grown-ups would lean out their windows watching us kids, never afraid to scold any of us, even if they didn't know us by name.

So we stayed in line, rarely doing anything that could have us sent inside and away from the fun. My best friend was my cousin Felicia; she and I paired off and usually went in our own direction away from the older girls who didn't want anything to do with little sisters. All the boys had a crush on Felicia, the poster child for ghetto beauty: light skin, hazel eyes, sandy hair. Unfortunately, she lacked the confidence usually afforded someone with her pedigree, while I, the darkest, shortest, and nappiest of the bunch, expected any boy to feel lucky to get my attention.

I never knew where the confidence actually came from. Looking back, I see it was probably listening to my mother rage against color-struck, self-hating blacks and the ignorant way that, a hundred years postslavery, they still valued those who appeared closer to white in hopes of removing all melanin from their family trees. My mother, who had trophy-girlfriend looks, wound up hating the limitations her physical appearance placed on her, eventually giving up both makeup and men. One time when Felicia and I babysat two younger girls in the neighborhood, one her shade, the other mine, the more outspoken of the two announced in that snobby way that can make you immediately hate children, "Let's play house. Felicia will be my mother because she is light skinned and pretty like me." I stopped myself from slapping some sense into that poor child's head, but she wasn't the only person I'd come across who thought like that. There existed and still exists a world of self-hating blacks of all ages and from all walks of life.

Once, when my mother showed up at my school unannounced, looking fly in a mod dress hand sewed from a Vogue pattern, all the kids stared and whispered about this beautiful movie star. Those same kids fell out of their seats in shock when the teacher announced that she was my mother. Nobody ever thought I belonged to my mother or with my sisters. Not only were they shades lighter with long hair and long legs, they were always pulled together and well composed, while I was the scruffy kid with ashy legs and scratches on my face from all the fights I started.

Eventually the boys crushed out on Felicia transferred their affections elsewhere, since her shyness couldn't find anything to say to them. This left an indelible impression on me to be myself no matter what—especially when it came to boys. That experience along with my mother's constant haranguing that "looks will only get you so far" cemented my understanding that I needed to be an individual.

Had our mothers known that at eight and nine years old we were running the streets with boys till 3:00 a.m., they would have banned us from ever visiting our grandmother again. But we knew better than to risk freedom with truth. Besides, all we did was play hide-and-go-seek, tag, and hopscotch and listen as the more boisterous boys played the dozens with one another's feelings. Occasionally we sought out our grandmother at whatever house her floating card game resided that night. Just our appearance assured us some money to get out of her face so she could concentrate on her game. If it was a good night and my grandmother won at cards or hit the number, we were tromped to the grocery store in the morning and all allowed to pick out our own boxes of cereal. I loved Cap'n Crunch or Trix, but Renee always chose puffed rice even though it had no sugar and no prize. As the middle child, Renee learned to take the smallest portion, the cheapest treat, and to never complain.

But if my grandmother lost at her card game, which happened more often than the wins, we six stood around the barren kitchen as she sliced government cheese and Spam, the international mystery meat, extolling the virtues of this feast. Nonetheless, I preferred going to my grandmother's house because, unlike my mother, she always had food and knew how to cook. She also didn't mind if we kids made noise and got on her nerves. My grandmother had left her birthplace of Rockingham, North Carolina, at three years old, but she retained the ability to throw down on some Southern food.

The official story about my mother was that my grandmother remained chaste until the age of twenty-eight, when she was either raped or sweet-talked out of her virginity by some "high yella" no-good man. After my mother's birth, my formerly virginal grandmother returned to New York and bore six other children by five or six different men, depending on who is telling the story. Her having been raped would explain the distance between her and her oldest child, my mother. They never managed to forge any familial bond, always shadow-boxing their discomfort and disappointment around each other.

Any real or imagined slight on the part of my grandmother inspired angry words from my mother, because it was a harsh reminder of the childhood she sacrificed in order to care for her younger siblings. At one point, when my ten-year-old mother was left at home with my grandmother's newest child, my baby aunt became gravely ill and had to be rushed to the hospital by my young mother. After the baby was pronounced dead, my mother had to identify her little sister's body. She never forgave her mother for not being there.

Years later, I came to understand the baggage between my mother and grandmother. I found it hard to reconcile the man-crazy party-girl mother of seven who'd been callous enough to abandon six for others to raise with the grandmother I knew. My aunt Bonita, my grandmother's youngest, became the only child my grandmother actually raised or "chose," something my mother would loudly remind her of at family gatherings.

My grandmother loved her grandchildren and always liked having us around, even if she complained about it, a fact that only caused my mother further pain and resentment. Memories of the Catholic orphanage where my mother entered adolescence lived in our photo album in the black-and-white picture of her in a pressed white dress, seated among other students and sandwiched between two poker-faced, frowning nuns. My mother, a self-described atheist, nevertheless had all three of her daughters baptized just in case the God who she informed us did not exist in fact did.

I could be a pretty outspoken troublemaker, and my hard head and sassy mouth assured a soft behind from the constant beatings I received as punishment. When pushed, I could not help myself from saying the one thing that guaranteed a class-A ass whipping. A more cautious child would have stopped before the threat of a beating graduated into a promise, but that was not me.

And once I knew a whipping was on the horizon, I set about earning a raw hide with all my might. After all, the beating would not get worse—it would be the same—but I needed assurance that it be well earned. My smart mouth sank me further and further into trouble, usually with my grandmother, who could not stand children to be out of control, but I didn't care because she was old, and her punishment paled in comparison to the beatings from my mother.

For years, I was the only grandchild ever to receive my grandmother's beatings—an honor I thoroughly deserved. The Stephanie tale recounted round the dinner table at large functions, guaranteed to send family members into hysterics, told of an infamous nonbeating. My grandmother and Aunt Bonita took the six of us to Central Park for the day—Cecilia, Renee, Deborah, me, Felicia, and Daniel. On the subway train home, I thought it appropriate to swing from the poles while fellow riders shot my aunt and grandmother judgmental looks reserved for people who failed to control their children in public. As if it wasn't bad enough that by the end of the day we resembled ragamuffin ghetto children.

Embarrassed, my grandmother yelled, "Stephanie, get off that pole before I beat you."

The only thing worse than embarrassment was shame, which sent me off running in the direction of more trouble. My grandmother's face knotted in rage. Not only did I stay on the pole, I hopped the length of the train swinging from pole to pole like a monkey let loose from the zoo. My sisters, Felicia, Deborah, and Daniel watched in surprise. I usually depended on my charm to narrowly avoid punishment, but this time there was no mistaking my defiance. My behavior was a gigantic middle finger held up to authority and anyone who judged me.

My grandmother lunged after me, but she was in her sixties and I was seven, all legs and arms. "Wait till we get home!" she screamed as I slid past her. "You are going to get a beating."

The others joined in adding their hoots and hollers, taunting me about the smackdown awaiting me. Knowing that my fate was sealed and punishment was imminent, I acted a fool.

My grandmother narrowed her eyes. "Go ahead, because I am going to whup your little ass when we get home."

Even Felicia, normally game for my risk taking, shook her head at me, warning. On the way home from the train station the taunts grew louder.

"Momma going to kill Stephanie. She ain't but a minute anyway so at least it'll be quick." Aunt Bonita laughed.

"It's gonna hurt 'cause Grandma is mad," Deborah added.

"You did it this time, girl, Grandma is breathing fire," Cecilia noted.

"I don't care. I been beat before," I shouted at them.

"Stephanie, maybe you should just be quiet," Renee warned me, always the more protective of my two sisters.

As we approached the house, Cecilia, the first grandchild and the noted favorite, offered to fetch the belt. That's when the reality hit me: I had a serious ass whipping coming. All the kids and my aunt gathered in the living room, waiting for my grandmother to deliver on her promise. She had been quiet since exiting the train, which meant she was fuming mad.

"Get my belt." My grandmother's voice was barely audible; it sent the kids scurrying, competing for her weapon of ass destruction. I backed away toward the open bedroom between the living room and kitchen.

"Don't go all quiet now. You had a lot to say on that train," my aunt reminded me.

Someone handed my grandmother the belt, and I was off, a lightning-flash image diving under the king-size bed in the next room.

"Catch her!" my grandmother yelled to the kids.

They all tried, but I had a head start and burrowed under the heavy bed, sharing space with years-old size-thirteen shoes and sneakers belonging to my jailbird uncle Gerald. He'd been in jail a few years, and I promise you that no one had bothered to dust under the bed since his incarceration. Years of dust balls the size of feral cats assaulted me along with the stench of my uncle's feet.

"Get her from under there," my grandmother, now getting her second wind, shouted.

The bed shook as five sets of arms pulled—with the exception of Felicia's—desperate to expose me hidden below, to send me to my fate. I felt hands snatching dirty, dust ball–covered shoes from under the bed. I grabbed the springs from the underside of the bed and held on for dear life, pushing my feet through the holes.

"Get her," my grandmother ordered again, but I could not be budged.

They moved the bed from side to side, swinging my frightened body in the air. It was them against me, and although I refused to worry about my grandmother, I began to fear the collective group.

Alone in my world, I screamed out, "Nobody loves me, nobody cares," and as these words tumbled from my mouth, in that moment I believed they were true. They, the group that formerly included me, laughed out loud, ridiculing my truth.

They dove onto the bed, pulling the mattress off, like rabid, hungry dogs trying to uncover me, and I screamed, this time louder, "Nobody loves me, nobody cares." I cried out, begging to be heard, because at that moment, I truly felt alone and unloved.

Suddenly my grandmother shouted, "Stop!" She paused. "Leave her alone."

And everything shifted, and the threat of the beating was no more. The bed ceased shaking, and I let go and dropped to the floor, exhausted and relieved.

"She's not getting a beating," the group cried out in disappointment. "It's not fair."

"Girl, get out from under the bed and get out of my face." But my grandmother was laughing.

I emerged from under the bed, dirty and triumphant, the kids sneering at me, teasing, "Nobody loves me, nobody cares." But I didn't mind what they thought, because I had done the impossible—I had talked myself out of the harsh punishment I deserved. I had made my grandmother laugh instead.

Bed-Stuy, Brooklyn

The apartment we lived in the longest was on Patchen Avenue and Jefferson Street in the Bedford-Stuyvesant section of Brooklyn. In 1970, before Spike Lee and gentrification deemed Bed-Stuy hip, it was home to people of all income levels, but particularly those struggling on life's bottom rung. In the early seventies Bed-Stuy had been hit hard by the loss of many of its young men to the debacle of the Vietnam War. I remember visiting neighbors who had lost sons in the war. And many others returned to the neighborhood wounded and broken and succumbed to drugs and drink. The sadness and rage of Vietnam darkened the spirits of the families, and many were unable to recover their joy or hope for themselves or surviving family members. I remember adults in my neighborhood arguing that it wasn't our war. I had no idea what this meant, but I connected to the powerlessness of my neighbors. A dark pall fell over Bed-Stuy after the war, and it would be years before it began to lift.

For six years that apartment was home to us. Finally, we had some stability, and we three sisters were able to form lasting friendships and put down roots. I feared the day we'd return home to find our mother packing, but that would be years later, and then it would be a life-changing move. Instead of moving, my mother insisted on redecorating with alarming regularity. It became normal to return after a weekend with family to find the entire apartment repainted and redecorated. Since my mother could not change where we lived, she focused on making it habitable.

One Sunday we came home to find six rooms painted in different colors. Renee discovered all six leftover colors splashed on the walls of her bedroom. After my mother fell asleep, Renee broke down and cried. At twelve, Renee faded into the background, invisible next to me, the youngest, with my white princess bedroom set with gold trim and freshly painted pink walls, and Cecilia, whose blue bedroom had a brass bed and matching dressers. Renee's boxy, unpainted furniture solidified her place as the last to be considered. Unlike me, the spoiled baby, and Cecilia, the moody eldest, Renee made life easier for our mother, becoming her confidant and assistant. She never complained or demanded more for herself. She had the ability to think about someone other than herself during what is usually the most selfish time of a person's life, childhood. But even in adulthood, Renee's version of our childhood is painted a rosy pink while both mine and Cecilia's are considerably darker. My mother was forever using funds that should have been allocated for more practical purposes (like food and clothes) on non-survival items such as paint and books. I joked that if books were edible I would have never known hunger. But I did know hunger.

My two sisters and I, all early readers, learned from my mother how to subsist within the pages of a book. Cecilia loved romance, Renee thrillers, and I loved drama, romance, and nonfiction. My mother read everything, from Truman's autobiography to bestsellers to books on sociology and literature. She loved words, their delicate ability to describe events and emotions, tying people and things together. We four all craved a world outside the walls of the ghetto where we dwelled, so we saw the lives in books as freedom. It was freedom from the limitations that threatened to suffocate our dreams.

On any given evening the four of us could be found in our separate rooms, escaping into our books. I checked out by daydreaming that I was the protagonist in the story, that it was my life readers were fascinated with. I stretched for a bigger, brighter landscape because poverty made me aware of my insignificance in the world.

By the sixth grade I had become the librarian's pet, called on to review the latest additions to the school's collection. The fact that a grownup trusted my opinion added to my love of reading. Being called out of class to meet with the librarian felt special, and I wanted so badly to grow up to be a writer so that she could read my books.

For a time my mother worked at Barnes and Noble on Fifth Avenue and would buy me two books a week on her employee discount. No matter how many books the library or my mother gave me, my appetite for words always left me hungering for more. Eventually I turned to my mother's overstuffed bookshelves to satisfy my cravings. Instead of Judy Blume, M. E. Kerr, Norma Klein, Paula Danziger, or Louise Meriwether, who offered a more watered-down version of childhood than the one I lived, I found Trudy Baker's *Coffee, Tea, or Me?*, Helen Gurley Brown's *Sex and the Single Girl*, and Jacqueline Susann's *Valley of the Dolls*, among others. At first, my mother demanded I read more age-appropriate books, but eventually she saw that neither she nor the library could provide materials fast enough for the rate at which I consumed them. I needed the constant escapism books afforded me. My mother gave up fighting my need to satisfy my hunger for words.

My seventh-grade book report on world history had me covering the six-hundred-page epic *Inside the Third Reich* by Albert Speer, which was so far over my head. My classmates rolled their eyes at my choice, not to mention the dictionary-sized book, but it fascinated me to enter a world so relentlessly brutal and horrendous. It made my mother's demand for silence and my growling stomach seem selfish by comparison. How could I complain of hunger or not having new shoes or fashionable clothes when people had been ripped out of their homes in the light of day, forced onto train rides with certain endings? Reading that book solidified my belief: Jesus was not available for those in real need like me. He reminded me of the boys in school who only sought me out when I ignored them, whereas if I gave any indication of a real desire, they'd disappear or, worse, call me out and embarrass me in front of my friends. Our male deity was nothing more than a phantom whose picture, with outstretched arms and a glowing halo, completed the Black Trinity in my grandmother's home, along with photographs of Martin Luther King Jr. and John F. Kennedy, whose support of blacks gave him honorary status.

My earliest memories were of lack, of wanting, of not having enough, which eventually internalized into not being enough. As the youngest of three girls, I wore clothes that were passed to me by my sisters. This would not have been such a nightmare, except my sisters had long legs and long arms, and everything about me was short, as if my extremities had been hacked off, like a traditional Japanese coffee table. Wearing other people's clothing made it difficult for me to define my individuality. My mother's concern that I had clean clothes to wear never took into account middle-class issues of style or attractiveness. My body became a worn pallet of tastes and ideals that were not mine, and so I chose to define myself with words, first in the pages of books, then with my own.

At age seven I began to transcribe my daydreams onto paper, telling a less painful version of the life I led. Writing allowed me to create the world as I longed to see it, not as the flawed and disappointed one I inherited. My recurring fantasy was that my "real family" would rescue me from the strangers who kept me locked up in this emotionally abstinent, poverty-stricken family, where I wasn't allowed to make noise or eat dessert. I wanted the perfect life, to be at home among kings and castles, and if I couldn't make it real in person, I'd do it on paper.

While I was aware of my mother's love for her three daughters, and even believed I was the favorite, I never actually heard her utter the words *I love you*. My belief had more to do with feeling that she was grooming me to be a younger version of herself, while she allowed my sisters to be themselves—within reason. Who wouldn't prefer a mini version of herself over those who are different? My mother didn't touch us or verbalize her love; for her love meant showing up every day, working two jobs, giving us a roof over our heads, and making sure we knew how to read. She needed our minds to expand even at the expense of our stomachs. Unlike her mother, she kept all of us together through tremendous hardships. We were always one paycheck away from homelessness, and although she never said it, I could sense her loneliness as she curled up in bed with only hardbound books to comfort her. Yet she never allowed us to live in the projects or filled our lives with a revolving door of Daddy substitutes. For her, these indications of love were stronger than spoken words.

But she herself was still a scared, broken child who had never had a mother she could count on or a childhood, which she insisted on giving to us. The first time my mother heard someone say they loved her, it was a man-child horny to release a hard-on, leaving her pregnant with her first child at age sixteen.

Years later, just like my mother and sisters, I heard my first-ever *I love you* from a teenage boy who expected those words to be the "open sesame" to surrendering my virginity to him. Maybe my refusal came from being the third of three girls and having the vantage point of seeing my older sisters seduced by the words *I love you* from boys I considered undeserving of them. Then, as now, thousands of love-starved, fatherless girls relinquished their virginity for what they believed would be the healing power of romantic love, and were left used up and betrayed. That first boy's profession of love failed to win my cherry, as did the second's and third's. As unfamiliar as I was with love, I still knew it was more than a bargaining tool and shouldn't carry such a heavy tax.

As hard as my mother worked to make sure we had the childhood she didn't, she was unable to give us the affection, patience, or love we needed. Raising three girls alone didn't allow her the luxury of addressing all of our emotional, material, physical, and educational needs, and many things got left behind. My mother was afraid to show affection for fear it would weaken our defenses, and the world would chew us up and spit us out. She believed her restraint would ultimately make us strong. She had no idea that hugs and verbal professions of love would have given us warrior strength and power.

I knew my sisters and I were a burden on my overworked, underpaid, lonely young mother. I didn't realize it as a child, but my mother had dreams once, dreams that had nothing to do with being nursemaid to three ungrateful daughters, dreams not limited to the six-block radius we called home, slaving away at some minimum-wage job. And now her dreams for us stretched far beyond the limitations and poverty in which she had been brought up. She insisted we learn of worlds outside the boundaries of our neighborhood.

My sisters and I were enrolled at the Henry Street Settlement Abrons Arts Center on the Lower East Side. Cecilia and Renee were placed in the drama department at my mother's insistence, but against their wills, while I joined the modern dance class. We went to Henry Street twice a week. Every Thursday after school, we three took the L train across the river, my sisters complaining loudly and often about having to endure such a hardship.

I, however, loved leaving Brooklyn, crossing over the river, and seeing the foreign land inhabited by older Jewish and Polish immigrants. Unlike our neighborhood, which was all black, this area fascinated me because of the rare diversity I found outside my books. I wanted to be transported away from all the limitations glaring out from our life in Bed-Stuy so I could believe that I could be more.

Thanks to arts grants, on Saturdays we were taken free of charge from Henry Street to cultural events around the city: the opera, a Mikhail Baryshnikov performance, the Joffrey Ballet, and Broadway theater. In the summer Shakespeare in the Park came to our neighborhood, and all the noise quieted down for those few hours. Everybody around me wanted more and refused to take this tiny slice of culture for granted.

The one friendship of my mother's that survived time was based solely on geographic proximity. Our downstairs neighbors, the Arnettes, became an extended family. Gwen, Earl, and their children Sharon and Junior were the ideal nuclear family and lived the life I dreamed about. Yes, I wanted to be a princess in a castle, but the Arnettes' life was so much more accessible.

Junior was one year younger than me, and as the only children in our age group in the building, we became friends out of pure necessity. Childhood was lonely enough without being isolated. Junior would have preferred a boy his age with a good sense of humor and a love of violent war games who didn't cry or know everything. But because we had working parents, our freedoms were limited to the world inside the building. Since there were very few children in the eight apartments, we were more than aware of the need to keep this friendship from coming apart at the seams. This was before yuppie playdates and parents who shuttle kids to the homes of their friends. Even when we got on each other's nerves we knew that as soon as our homework was done, we'd seek out one another. Junior's ever-growing collection of G.I. Joes needed dolls to torture, and at thirteen his sister was way past her Barbie stage, preferring to be fashionable and boy crazy like Cecilia. Sharon and Renee started out as best friends, born only a few days apart, but as Sharon matured, she abandoned her tomboyish ways in favor of presenting a more feminine side to her male admirers. You'd have to tie Renee down to make her wear anything girlie, while Cecilia and Sharon lived for the attentions of the opposite sex. Renee's losing her best friend to her older sister caused a fissure in the relationship between my sisters, one I'm not sure ever healed completely. So when I went down to Junior's house, Sharon usually disappeared to my house or locked herself in the bedroom with Cecilia away from us "loud brats."

The other, less noble reason I sought out a friendship with Junior was pure survival. Unlike our house, where food choices were limited or nonexistent, the Arnettes always had plenty to eat. I carefully timed my visits to coincide with afternoon snack hour, usually a tasty TV dinner Earl Senior brought home from his job at a local public school. Luckily, we qualified for free hot breakfast and lunch at school, but by the time we got home our stomachs held no memories of the state-sanctioned fare they fed free-lunch students in the cafeteria. Afternoon snacks were a luxury we could not afford. I tried to play it casual, like it was a coincidence, but once Junior figured out my real intentions, he began to block me at the door, insisting I return after his snack time. Apparently it didn't matter that he had more food than he could ever eat; no one liked being taken advantage of, even out of desperation. I had no idea how many times this scenario would play out in my life. Nothing equals the embarrassment of being caught using a friend for food.

One summer was magical because my mother began to hang out with a group of artists who lived in Manhattan. Suddenly we were no longer confined to the inner city of Brooklyn. The L train shuttled us to a whole other life on a more regular basis. We went to gallery openings and were photographed by artists. We saw off-Broadway theater and hung out in recording studios listening to singers lay tracks.

Because my mother's menial secretary jobs were constantly changing, so were her friends. She didn't see a point to putting up with a lot of nonsense when she could get an equally under-paid and underappreciated job somewhere else. The people my mother befriended were a convenience of work or school. We were too young to comprehend the transient nature of life on the bottom of the food chain. My mother didn't seem capable of nurturing her friendships past a pink slip, so there was a revolving door of aunties and uncles. We never understood the regular dismissal of people from my mother's life. Because of her hardscrabble upbringing, she had no tools for maintaining intimacy and close friendships.

When I was eight years old, my mother and aunt managed to send all six of us older children off to summer camp for a month. This was their freedom song. It was some version of the Fresh Air Fund that provided camp for those less fortunate and was my mother's first summer of peace in eight years. Here we were, roughneck city kids let free in the great outdoors.

But three days into camp I partnered with another future juvenile delinquent and got kicked out for throwing rocks—albeit at a window. Although I didn't think I could get booted from the wilderness for tossing rocks, I did.

My mother must have wanted to scream when the month-long retreat she had planned was cut short because her youngest behaved like a wild animal, forgetting every etiquette lesson she had taught me. On the bus ride back to the city I studied and studied the one postcard she had sent me at camp, more open and revealing of her feelings than the mother I knew in person. She wrote in pen that she loved me.

Wow! My mother actually said *I love you* on the page. I wondered if things would be different when I got home. Would I be met with open arms and pronouncements of a new flow-ing love?

Looking back, I wonder if my real motivation for getting thrown out of camp was to see if my mother had changed, softened, like the words in her letter. But that never changed. We were a family in which it was safer to write down feelings than even to whisper them aloud. Still, in spite of my mother's initial anger and resentment at my early homecoming, I loved having her to myself that summer. It was the first time that I didn't have to share my mother with my sisters.

No matter how hard my mother stretched her budget, it proved inadequate when it came to feeding and clothing three girls of different sizes. We were always behind on some bill or another. We knew this, since we were directed to answer the bill collectors' phone calls and assure them that our mother would call as soon as she came home. And of course there were the times our phone, electricity, or gas was shut off without any warning. We'd arrive from school only to find our home absent a working television, refrigerator, or stove.

Because my mother didn't finish high school, her earning potential was limited. Eventually she took her GED, which helped but didn't elevate her earnings enough to make a real difference in our lifestyle. With a limited education, my mother wasn't able to catch up with the impossible overhead, and she found creative ways around her numerous financial issues. When she could not afford the growing utility bills, she began to use her daughters' clean credit records to put the utilities in our names. The phone was in Cecilia's name when she was ten.

My mother came from a world where it was impossible to look at the big picture or long-term goals. She could not worry how destroying our credit ratings as children would affect us as adults. Her concerns were more immediate: she needed to provide us with lights and gas and electricity without a sizable deposit or late fee added to an already impossible balance. In the world she came from, tomorrow would bring only new worries, concerns, and crises, so she became expert at dodging the minefields of poverty confronting her today and avoiding problems that could be put off until tomorrow. She learned to borrow from Peter in order to pay Paul, juggling one bill's late notice to stop another utility from being turned off. For my mother, survival mode was the norm. She functioned as a soldier in her personal war against the massive system that threatened to take every human right away at a moment's notice.

When one of us came down with an illness, she couldn't afford the luxury of tucking us into bed with a warm serving of Campbell's chicken noodle soup. Instead, she'd bundle us up and send us to school. If our symptoms were serious enough to have her called at work, she'd coax a relative to step in and take care of us. Often, we three hid our illnesses from my mother, conscious of the domino effect it would have on her well-being.

Of the six of my grandmother's living children, my mother was perceived as the poorest. Even my aunt Rita, who depended on social security and welfare, seemed to have a more steady cash flow than us. Whenever we went to her apartment, she'd always scare up enough money to send us to the local Chinese take-out for shrimp fried rice and fried chicken wings with a side of sweet sauce, something we rarely got to do at home. We ate like royalty in the dingy four-room flat above the storefront temple on Church Avenue where my aunt and her husband raised their three children.

Unlike my aunts and uncles, who allowed themselves to enjoy the fruits of their hard work, my mother poured whatever resources she could muster into self-improvement. Our other family members worked forty hours a week at jobs where they'd never get rich, so they enjoyed their downtime by cooking big dinners, drinking rum and Cokes, listening to music, and dancing. My mother, my aunt Susie, and my uncles John and Sonny once had a social club along with the Arnettes and a few others, and they'd throw dances together. But after a short time, my mother slipped back into her shell, taking refuge in a good book. She was constantly taking classes at local colleges, which were paid for either by her employer or the government, working toward bettering herself and seeking a rabbit hole to slip into, in the hopes of improved circumstance. Even today my mother is a college student.

The cost of our rent hovered above my mother's budget, but she refused to reside in the projects with residences "stacked on top of each other like roaches," as she'd describe them. She wanted better for herself, and she simply didn't have a lot of patience for people who didn't want more out of life. She never followed the trends or did what other people found acceptable. When all the neighborhood girls were fashionable in inexpensive plastic jelly shoes, easily purchased for five bucks, my mother insisted we all wear sturdy Fred Braun penny loafers. She wanted to protect our feet from poorly made shoes that would ruin them forever. Our shoes definitely did not earn cool points among friends. They looked podiatric and lacked fashion sense, not to mention we would have been able to have more than two pairs of shoes a year had she bent on this rule of hers, but my mother was incapable of bending. It was as if she believed that buying us better shoes would guarantee us entrance into a better life. She took the maxim that you can tell all about a person by the kind of shoes they wear to heart, insisting on quality. Unfortunately, few in our neighborhood agreed with our mother; most chose style over substance each and every time, and we stood by, longing to be down with them.

My mother not only didn't believe in God, she considered his entire existence a sham. This great Almighty who could turn water into wine and part seas had failed to rescue unwanted, unloved children, so by the time we came along my mother refused to believe. Being partially raised in a Catholic orphanage made her run in the opposite direction when it came to devoting any of her life to the mythical Savior. She had spent years being brutalized and repressed, all in the name of a merciful God who failed to show her any kindness or mercy. Having God forced upon her led to a détente when it came to religion. If God didn't bother her, she wouldn't bother God.

Nonetheless, this did not stop my mother from sending her three girls off to church on random Sundays when we didn't visit relatives. Weekends were usually my mother's rare time for solitude, away from us and the workload facing her on the coming Monday. On those Saturdays when we failed to go to relatives, my mother handed Renee money to take us to the movies. It didn't matter that Cecilia was the oldest; Renee was the most reliable. My mother never questioned the appropriateness or long-term effects of the blaxploitation movies she sent us to; *Coffy*, *Foxy Brown*, *Five on the Black Hand Side*, and *Mandingo* were a few of the titles we saw. We'd hover outside the theater along with a group of underage regulars waiting for an adult to purchase our tickets since we were too young to see these sex and violence features. All the movies played with a double-feature horror film, so my mother would have four hours of freedom from motherhood.

Then on Sunday mornings my mother awoke to three girls who wanted to make noise and be kids and, well, she couldn't handle that. She made us dress, gave us each a dollar for the collection plate, and sent us off to church. Within a three-block radius were half a dozen churches, and she didn't care which one we chose as long as it had a three-hour service. She wanted to be free of her children and didn't care if she had to relinquish them to God to make that happen. Of course, she made sure to remind us that God did not exist and that we should pay attention to how many times the collection plate was passed around so we'd see that this was a greedy hustle. Church was commerce, plain and simple, another way for the crooked establishment to get money out of unsuspecting poor people in need. The more needy the people, the more they gave in the hopes that the great and mysterious God would answer their prayers and help their lives.

We always kept our eyes on the collection plates, hoping a ten or twenty would slip into our laps as it passed us. My sisters and I sat through many services, focused on the dollar in our pocket and the treats we would buy ourselves when church ended. Never once did it occur to us to put the offering in the plate as it passed. A dollar was a lot of money to us, and since our mother didn't seem to believe in God, why should we give up our money to him?

Few of my relatives ever went to church or talked about God. Part of my family had been raised Jewish, and my first cousin Daniel had even been bar mitzvahed. Few people are aware of the black Jewish people who exist in America. They are minorities within a minority. Many were born into the Jewish faith, while some converted to it later, often through marriage. In my family the ties to Jewish heritage came through both blood and marital relations. The head of my relatives' synagogue was himself a distant relative who seemed to handpick the parts of ancient Judaism that best served him, parts that are no longer accepted by the masses, including the outdated ones about having more than one wife. He was a small, intense man who never showed an ounce of humor. One of his wives never left the house because she weighed more than four hundred pounds. Whenever I was forced to go to their house, I would get physically ill at the sight of that obese woman trapped in a bed in the center of her apartment, where her sons, along with the second wife's children, would scurry around waiting on her. It wasn't just the weight but also the powerlessness of her situation that disturbed me. Food had become her jailer long before I understood the power of eating. I believed the cause of her appetite had something to do with sharing a man whose size and temperament were inadequate and punishing. She couldn't stop eating, and her family wouldn't stop enabling her by bringing her the food she couldn't get herself. One day I would relate more to her than any other member of my family.

Religion was seen as a weak person's crutch, not to mention that the majority of my family preferred to party or gamble on Saturdays and had no interest in waking up on Sunday mornings for God or anyone else. We were what you might call heathens when it came to organized religion, and nobody had any interest in changing. Yet almost all the relatives hung a picture of white Jesus in their homes just in case we were wrong and God really did exist. The fact that Jesus was nailed to the cross in these pictures could have been our way of relating to at least one white person in our lifetimes; after all, we were natural-born sufferers.

After church my sisters and I would always walk to the bodega that was the farthest from our apartment so that we could eat our ill-gotten treats before we reached home. I often saved the majority of my money for school, so I could go to the candy store with my friends who always had money for sugary treats. It made me feel like one of the "haves" when I would show up for school on Monday with money in my pocket and able to buy some junk food like my friends. I had spent so much time salivating after the treats of my classmates that I loved inspiring that kind of envy in others. A favorite wintertime snack in our inner-city school was Now and Later candy. We'd sneak it onto the radiator, eating it when it was warm enough to spread like taffy on your tongue. How many times had I watched the other students laying the watermelon, apple, grape, lemon, or chocolate on the radiator? With my attention focused on the candy, I had trouble concentrating on schoolwork.

Monster in the Family

Of all our relatives' homes, we preferred to spend time at Uncle John's, my mother's younger brother. Uncle John worked on Wall Street as a stockbroker, and he was the only success story on my shaky family tree. He had been raised in foster care, and at eighteen he escaped by shipping off to the army. After his tour of duty, Uncle John returned stateside, used the GI Bill to go to college, and wound up in the money. He married and had two children, both girls, and would eventually have a third.

Uncle John was the only one of my grandmother's six children who seemed able to sustain a marriage, which even the youngest among us found fascinating. We loved his house because he and his wife, Aunt Clarissa, ran a stable, organized household. She clearly wasn't one of my grandmother's children. Aunt Clarissa had been raised in a loving two-parent household and took pity on our lack of knowledge about things she considered normal, like holiday traditions that did not include children drinking Manischewitz Concord grape wine.

At Christmastime Aunt Clarissa taught us the ritual of leaving cookies out for Santa, along with a glass of milk. When her young children awoke on Christmas morning, they would find half-eaten cookies, an almost-empty milk glass, and a note from Santa thanking them for being thoughtful, good girls. My sisters, cousins, and I were all blown away because if we were lucky enough to have a cookie at our house it would have gotten eaten immediately, Santa be damned.

Uncle John and Aunt Clarissa introduced us to other things outside of our normal reach: sit-down restaurants instead of the rare outing to a fast-food place. Occasionally my mother could afford to take us to the local Chinese restaurant, but eating out was an uncommon treat for us. Every Saturday morning they went to the Buccaneer Diner in Queens, and when we went along we could order anything we wanted off the menu, which made me feel like Eloise at the Plaza. I remember my uncle telling me to slow down because I ate at a breakneck speed more fitting for the new guy in prison than a child at a local eatery. I worried that someone was playing a trick on me, and at any moment this incredible food would be snatched away, like a scene out of a Hans Christian Andersen fairy tale.

After a while I came to understand that this was just the way my uncle and his family lived, and that if I was good, I would be invited back. Being "good" usually meant following the rules of adults, even though these rules were subject to change depending on any number of circumstances, including the weather or a monthly cycle or a new boyfriend.

For my sisters and me, our burdens lessened when we went to Uncle John's house. The money worries, limited portions of food, and the idea of food as optional were nonexistent. We could always have extra at Uncle John's. He and his family could buy anything they wanted, go anywhere, and do anything. What may have seemed normal to more than half the population was a rare and somewhat amazing occurrence to us three.

We never mentioned our bleak financial picture or told Uncle John that we only ate this well when we were with them. My sisters and I felt protective of our mother, already the black sheep in our family, and we never shared our hunger situation with our relatives. My mother was too proud to take charity from her family, and we knew not to put her in that position. Her pride separated her from her siblings even more than the physical absence of my jailbird uncle Gerald separated him, as his consistent arrests revealed his preference for stability inside the prison system. Even among ourselves we rarely voiced the fact that our mother was cranky and mad and that she often forgot to feed us. It was as if we knew our mother was doing her very best and didn't want to send her over the edge, which always loomed too close anyway.

That day started like any other summer day. My sisters, my cousins Felicia and her older sister Deborah, and I were spending the weekend at my Uncle John's house helping to watch his kids, Jennifer and Monique. He and my aunt Clarissa had recently separated, with him living in a fancy apartment and being the weekend dad. Renee, Felicia, Deborah, and I went to nearby Flushing Meadows Corona Park to play with a group of growing boys who all seemed to have a crush on my sister. Cecilia was way too "mature" to hang out with us and went off on her own. On the way back to my uncle's we stopped to watch Renee beat one of the guys at handball.

By late afternoon my uncle and my sisters were in his bedroom smoking pot. I grew tired of observing others have fun and snatched the joint from my sister, put it between my lips, and attempted my first inhale.

"You are so grown," Cecilia laughed, her voice revealing her pleasure at my coughing fit.

"Oh, let her smoke," my uncle insisted, "she's always been fast."

I bristled at those words because I hated being called fast, since my comfort rested more closely with Barbie dolls than boys. I puffed away on the joint, letting it burn my throat as they watched, waiting for me to choke again, but I didn't.

Before my uncle's breakup with his wife, I had always been sent off to bed with his daughter Jennifer, who was six years younger than I was, and I hated it.

"Come on, Stephanie," Jennifer would taunt me when her parents sent her off to bed.

It didn't matter how much I threatened my little cousin, she continued to include me in her nightly exile. It never seemed to bother Felicia, who was a year younger than me, but I wanted to hang with my older sisters and be considered one of them. The last thing I wanted at twelve was to be relegated to the same bedtime as a six-year-old. This was my way of showing them that I was no longer in the same category as mere children. Felicia, who usually followed in my footsteps, stayed far away, signaling her disapproval at my behavior. She knew I was trying to prove I was old enough to hang because I hated being treated like a kid. I was almost thirteen, almost a woman, and I thought I was ready for marijuana, the bad-girl initiation. I had been around it for years, and I didn't see what the big deal was all about. The "Just Say No" campaign was years away, so I was blissfully ignorant of the possible repercussions of my actions.

Eventually my uncle got dressed and went carousing at his favorite haunt, the Playboy Club, leaving us to babysit his two young children. He worshipped that sacred key that allowed him entrance into the classiest sex club in the world. After he left, we girls laughed and played, dancing around, listening to music. All of us loved being together; it was one big playdate, six to eight of us piled into relatives' houses, a different place each weekend. Deborah and Felicia's younger brother Daniel refused to be stuck with eight girls, even though he was related, so he stayed at home with his mother.

The last thing I remember that night was the music, two sleeping children, five dancing girls, and laughter. We laughed outside the music, screaming, the sheer volume of our voices attempting to blend with Harold Melvin and the Blue Notes, *If you don't know me by now . . .* , our screeching tones killing cats all over the neighborhood. We were happy.

That night etched itself in my memory as my last night of childhood—pure, innocent, free. It would have been impossible to imagine that I would ever cease to feel the way I did in those moments. Being a part of a collective of girls who not only knew me but loved me, and who taught me how to make friends with joy, made me feel invincible in a way that only the young and unaffected can. But that night I traded in my freedom and naïveté for a prison of fear, betrayal, and self-loathing. Before daybreak, I would know what it was like to lose everything, including my place in my family.

Later on that night my uncle came home reeking of alcohol and fantasies of the beautiful women who allowed him to buy them overpriced drinks but offered no solution for his growing desires. Surely, he didn't think he was good enough to take one of the Playboy Bunnies home. Even if one of them said yes, he couldn't bring her to a house of seven girls ranging from ages one to sixteen. My uncle found me passed out on his bed, dreaming my last dream of peace, and carried me off, ensuring nightmares would greet me the next time night blanketed the sky. For him, a cold, hard thief, unapologetic partly due to the liquid courage coursing through his veins, I, his niece, his sister's child, didn't exist. I was a girl-child flat as a board, no obvious signs of maturity on my thin, underdeveloped frame. Compared with my bosomy, statuesque sisters, I considered myself gypped by the gods.

I thought the cold air woke me; the windows were open, blowing the summer night breeze, cooling the room. It took a moment to get my bearings, to understand my location and the realness of the moment. I felt large male hands rough between my legs, separating them from each other, and I froze.

"Stephanie, Stephanie," he whispered, trying to wake me alive in this nightmare, but I didn't answer.

Eventually he stopped calling my name, but I knew it was him. I knew my uncle John was attempting to take me places a child should never go, and I felt powerless to stop him. After all, it was my fault I fell asleep in his bed. I must have secretly wanted this. Maybe when I inhaled on that joint it was some kind of phallic signal to him that I was ready for this family rite of passage. My grandmother, mother, sisters, and even my uncle John had been raped as children. Did this mean that rape was supposed to be my destiny and I had no control over it? It didn't occur to me then that he had physically moved everybody else from his bed but chose to leave me—me with the body of a preteen boy.

He took off my underwear, looking to see if I would stir, but I didn't, I couldn't. Like a well-trained mutt, I played dead, hoping he would lose interest and go away. Instead, he got on top of me, positioning my body so it would be most receptive. Pushing my legs farther apart, he shoved his massive penis at me, prying for an opening, but I was a virgin, not even close to starting my period.

Having grown up without a God to pray to, or a father to reassure me, I shut my eyes tighter and willed him to go away. I had nowhere to go, no one to call out to, and so I slipped farther into myself, pretending to be invisible. I wanted him to leave me be, but his body felt like a leaden weight, and his stiff penis pushing into my unwilling vagina felt capable of ripping me in two. I told myself not to scream, believing if he knew I was awake it would somehow become real, even though I had no idea how it could become more real than this moment. Somehow my twelve-year-old mind convinced itself that if I kept my eyes closed and didn't see it, then maybe it wasn't actually happening. Maybe I could convince myself that this was nothing more than a bad dream.

After more forceful pushing and shoving and trying to penetrate me, he grew tired and stopped. He got up as I lay absolutely still, my body betraying no signs of life. I lay there, willing him to go away. But instead I felt the weight of him lowering himself back onto the bed, his body pressing into me. I wanted to scream, but I lost my voice; it too betrayed me in that moment. I knew I would be blamed; I was the fast one, I was anxious to grow up. I deserved this, they would say, I was too damn grown. But I didn't want this, I wanted anything but this. I silently begged for my mother's arms, a concrete expression of the love she withheld.

The sound of a jar being unscrewed brought me back into the room, into my body. I felt something sticky and slippery as he slathered Vaseline onto the entrance of my vagina, cold, wet, thick. His heavy man hands massaged the Vaseline into my privates for what felt like forever. Finally satisfied, he pulled my legs apart, climbed on top of me, and tried again to shove his penis into me. I was entering eighth grade, the shortest girl in the class, still under five feet, and here he was, five-foot-eleven and one hundred seventy-five pounds at least, again ripping apart my life with his bare penis. I cried inside where no one could hear, and I learned my best magic trick, how to be invisible. He grabbed his penis—thick, hungry—between his heavy hands and rammed it into me. The pain caused my body to lurch backward involuntarily, and I winced.

"Stephanie, you OK?" he asked, but I kept my eyes closed, unwilling to see his ugly face of betrayal.

Tears sprouted out of the corners of my eyes, a steady stream down the sides of my face, and I broke into two damaged pieces. I separated from my body and at that moment became forever twelve, forever wounded. He climbed back atop me, guiding his pulsating member past the opening, but he got stuck. It would not go any farther. My body would not allow him entry. He tried and tried until he tired once more and fell away.

Rising, he pulled on pajamas. I lay there silent, my voice frozen by betrayal, my eyes shut to the throbbing pain. He returned to the bed, stretched out, yawned, and fell into a deep sleep beside me as I stiffened, too scared to breathe. I believed that if I moved it would awaken him, and he would start again. So I lay next to my rapist and pretended to be OK, to be normal, to be dreaming.

At the first sign of daylight I slipped out of the bed, away from my family, my body still looming above me. It would be almost fifteen years before I would make my first attempt to reclaim myself and only after attempting to destroy myself first.

I sleepwalked through the next few days until I could return home, sidestepping my uncle and his attempts to be extra nice to me.

Never once did it occur to me to tell my mother what had happened. I couldn't. My mother housed a ready store of available anger to unleash on an unsuspecting passenger on a train, a slumlord, the drunken men who hung out on the corners commenting on the swell of her breasts beneath her clothes. She had the kind of anger made for prison, and I couldn't be the one she served a life sentence for defending. I knew she would not only believe me, but she would defend me to my uncle's death.

The other relatives, the ones with their hands out to my uncle, grateful for his generosity, would call me a liar, and my mother and I would be abandoned. She would be orphaned again if I told the truth, and so I kept my silence, not knowing that my uncle was not finished abusing the girls in my family.

From that fateful night, I refused to participate in my extended family. Sure, I went to events, smiled for pictures, babysat my younger cousins, but I was absent in all the ways that mattered, and I resented that nobody noticed. I grew to dislike my family gathered around my uncle, the crowned prince, celebrating him while reminding me how unruly I had suddenly become.

Ever since that moment, whenever I see a young girl being "grown" or suddenly acting out of control, I worry about who has "gotten at her." I always wonder who snatched her childhood away from her.

I watched and waited for the day I would be old enough never to need any of them again. I knew what rage tasted like, and I swallowed it whole, allowing it to peek out whenever no one was looking. I hated the very people who should have loved me, with the exception of my sisters and my mother and, of course, Felicia. But mostly I blamed myself and turned my rage inward.

Father's Day

A major distraction from my pain came when Renee, perfect, obedient daughter and protector of my mother, suddenly rebelled against her "don't ask, don't tell" policy regarding fathers. Cecilia alone had an occasional relationship with her father, whom we all knew and who had always been free to visit, even if he rarely took advantage of this privilege. She also was the only one who had her father's name, Sutton. Renee and I were Covingtons, like our mother and grandmother, and were never allowed to question this choice or ask about our fathers. My mother had taken on the role of both mother and father whether she liked it or not, and she would not stand for any suggestion that she was less than proficient at the job.

How my sister managed to find out enough information to track down her father remained a mystery to me. For all I knew, my father could have been anyone from the homeless vets clutching Mad Dog bottles on the corner to the mailman grunting as he trudged up our avenue loaded down with a sack full of bad news and bills. Seeing my mother's violent reaction after finding out Renee had reunited with her father was enough reason for me to keep my father sequestered in my fantasies. Besides, my luck with men made my fantasy father more attractive then a real one.

After discovering my sister's betrayal at not only finding her father but starting a relationship with him behind her back, my mother physically attacked my sister. She could not control her rage that Renee would want to be the daughter of someone who had caused her so much pain. Didn't this child understand that she kept her away from this man for a reason?

Instead of seeking my father out, I chose to regale the kids in the schoolyard with tales of my swashbuckling dad, whose career changed daily from world traveler to scientist to millionaire to CIA operative. He became everything I believed a father should be as I creatively explained away his absence with tall tales of him saving the world. What other reason would there be for a father abandoning his vulnerable daughter, unless a bigger, more dangerous mission forced him away from her?

In my neighborhood fathers went missing with regularity or never bothered to show up at all, so being fatherless never felt anything but normal. Of course I learned to envy those whose fathers cared enough to show up for the everyday events of their lives without fanfare, as if showing up were a simple thing. Felicia and Deborah had a spotty relationship with their father, who occasionally remembered his daughters, but they never seemed to mind or desire a closer bond with him.

Eventually my mother softened her stance and let Renee have regular visits with her father at his mother's house, four blocks away. He was that man the Temptations sang about, "Papa was a rolling stone," because he had children all over the place. Renee loved having siblings she'd occasionally meet at her grandmother's house. I was more than sated by my fantasy father and would have been horrified to learn that my absent parent had been spreading his seed all over the five boroughs and not saving the world.

One morning my mother woke me telling me to cook the one thing I knew how to make for dinner, spaghetti. Like a drill sergeant, she also instructed me on what to wear. My suspicions were aroused, but since my mother never did things the way you expected, I hadn't a clue what was going on.

That evening at around six, my mother, dressed in a light skirt and blouse, better than normal but nothing flashy, perked up as the doorbell rang. My sisters were instructed to go outside and play, which was an immediate giveaway, since we were never allowed to leave the house after my mother returned home at five o'clock.

In fact, my sisters and I stayed in the streets until fifteen minutes before my mother was supposed to arrive home every day, enjoying this small window of freedom in the outdoors like most of the other kids in the neighborhood. My mother thought our neighborhood too dangerous a place for her three girls, and so she banished us to the indoors. Renee and I would regularly drag Cecilia out of the local pool hall before our mother rounded the corner on her way home from work. My mother had justification for her paranoia, but it wasn't our fault that the danger lurking outside held more than a slight attraction. We weren't allowed to watch much television so most nights we snuck our heads out the window watching the spectacle of people having loud, rowdy fun. Behind her back, we'd complain that we wished our mother was like the others who drank to loosen up on Friday nights instead of chain-smoking and reading herself to sleep. Or like the moms who stayed home and collected welfare checks and welcomed their children's desires to flee outside. Or even the mothers who dated without fearing strange men around her children. We just wanted to be normal.

My mother opened the door to a short, dark, average man incapable of leaping tall buildings or owning a private island. He entered the living room carrying a box of chocolate-covered cherries. I still have a visceral, slightly nauseated reaction whenever I see a box of chocolate-covered cherries. My mother's voice softened, her smile grew wider, and her walk took on a sexy sway. I noticed. Stiff, conservative, with a West Indian accent, he asked harmless questions about my schooling while my mother gushed, displaying more emotion and interest than normal. We three sat down for dinner, my mother rattling off my achievements to this total stranger. It felt as if I had been dropped into an episode of the *Twilight Zone* with my mother acting unfamiliar. Neither my mother nor the company ever spoke one word about his reason for being there. The truth loomed, the eight-hundred-pound gorilla bobbing its head in front of us as we pretended to be oblivious to its presence. I paid close attention to my discomfort and sharp stabs around the stories they retold. I knew the answer, knew why he was there, even if no one confirmed it. His averageness offended me. No way was this man rescuing me from an uncertain future. Everything about him was studied, tentative, crisp, from his button-down shirt and houndstooth jacket with patches on the sleeves to his Bass Weejuns. As swiftly as he entered, he retreated when the meal was over, explaining an overflow of work still to be done. After my sisters came upstairs, bubbling over from the shock of sudden sovereignty, I avoided my mother.

I prepared for sleep devastated by this new reality that I was destined to live an underprivileged life. Up until that meeting I'd been able to comfort myself to sleep with visions of my swashbuckling absent parent swooping in and altering the course of my life in one magical moment. The kids who had always thought me inferior would be shocked to learn that I was not only rich and powerful but superior and loved. That night I tossed and turned, unable to find a comfortable position in my bed or in myself. I lay awake, saddled with the unpleasantness of this new reality. Would nothing ever go my way? Was there any point in dreaming myself into a new reality when this one constantly disappointed me? I screamed out in response to this trick life had played on me so soon after the other, greater pain. I didn't even realize my scream had been audible until my mother rushed in, offering me comfort, something I hadn't expected. She squeezed into bed beside me, and my body stiffened. My mother's touch was unfamiliar, unknown to me, and I couldn't handle the shock of it being offered in such a normal show of affection. I had waited almost twelve years for her to touch me and now, like my father, it had come too late.

"That man who came to dinner. Do you know who he is?" she questioned.

"Yes," I whispered, my voice barely audible.

"He's your father," she finished before I could respond.

Neither my mother nor I had any personal experience of a father, and yet I knew in that moment that whatever I expected, I would be disappointed. The word "father" had always been magical before tonight.

"He wants to get to know you," she pushed, her voice filled with anticipation and excitement. But to me his interest and mine were in opposition. He was another man shoving himself onto me without any thought as to what I would want or need.

Something in my nod must have triggered her concern, because she asked me to "give him a chance." My mother had never asked me anything in my entire life; she had always decided without argument or exception exactly what it was I needed. But there should be some kind of moratorium on absentee fathers suddenly appearing. At birth I needed a father, at five I still needed a father; ten, yes, but here I was about to be thirteen, crossing the threshold into young womanhood, and I believed I should be the one who made the decision about needing a father. On the recent night when my uncle violated me, my father forfeited the right to his paternity. My uncle knew that there was no man in my life to validate me or to care if he took what should have been mine to give. Did this stranger really expect twelve years of Father's Day cards along with my receptivity? Yes, I was angry. I had gotten used to the reality of being a fatherless daughter, and I did not want to relinquish it to the first unmet promise of a daddy-daughter reunion. How could my mother make me do this?

Even she didn't notice my recent withdrawal into myself. We four females in my house had always spent the majority of our time shut into our own separate rooms. My sisters and I learned to be independent even of one another. I had my own television, books, dolls, and toys to keep me busy, but I had never really liked the silence of being alone. I felt isolated and condemned in my room. Alone I daydreamed, creating a vision of my life free from outside interference.

My mother insisted on our independence and silence. She firmly believed children should be seen and not heard. That we should only speak when spoken to. If we failed to respect her need for quiet she could be a stern taskmaster, scaring us into submission. Unlike my cousins' houses where children were allowed to be their loud, noisy selves, our apartment became the last choice for weekend and summer gatherings. I often found myself pleading with Felicia to spend the weekend, but we were children, and everybody knew that the natural behavior of children was unacceptable in my mother's home.

After my rape, I came to love the solitude. I now found the comfort and safety within the bubble-gum-colored walls of my room that no longer felt available in the rest of the world. My favorite pastime was lying, staring at the ceiling, and dreaming of myself happy in an alternate universe. I couldn't wait until I was free to take control of my own life. I had already wrested control of my feelings away from the world. Away from my family. I refused to hurt, to feel pain, to let anyone close enough to be able to have the power to destroy me again. I promised myself that I would never again be caught off guard by believing I could be loved by a man. There would always be a chance that he would come bearing a darker, more sinister desire, and next time I would be prepared. So the last thing I wanted at this point was an average father offering me entrance to his ordinary life. I already had average, and what I needed was something spectacular, phenomenal, enough to make me forget. From that moment on my life became about forgetting. I did not want to want anything, especially something that could be snatched away like my sense of self and safety.

One Saturday afternoon the new man—my sperm donor, as my sisters and I coined him—took me to see *Jaws* in Times Square. I sat through the movie sneaking sideways glances at him, looking for similarities. He sat upright, stiff, staring straight ahead at the screen. He never once looked in my direction during the movie. Afterward he took me to Orange Julius for hot dogs and French fries. We were equally uncomfortable with each other. How do you go from being strangers to forming the familiar bond of parent and child? I had grown past the age of tolerance and obedience.

On the train ride back to Brooklyn he attempted to make conversation. To him I was a kid, but I had lived a different, less sheltered life than the young son he was raising. My halfbrother, Jasen, attended private school in lower Manhattan, doted on by two attentive parents. He lived my dream life, or so I thought. My father's kid references were from the vantage point of a privileged son seven years younger than me, but I believed he should instinctively know who I was and what interested me, so instead of conversation I offered curt oneword answers. I felt that this father wanted me to be outgoing, bubbly, and grateful for his attentions, not a sulky, smartass preteen who expected him to put in a little work for my affection.

Without him saying anything I knew that this outing had been a trial, and I had failed. To him I was little more than a ghetto rat to whom he had the misfortune of being related. I would soon learn that he had less patience than my mother. My father came from the West Indies, where boy children were revered and girls put to work serving these sacred sons. Had I been a boy my father might have felt some guilt over leaving me in the care of my mother, but even that is speculation.

My father never invited me to his house, never gave me a home number, instead insisting on keeping me and his life separate. For the longest time I felt like my father's dirty little secret that he shoved out of sight of his respectable life. When my father separated from his wife, things temporarily shifted in my favor. Eventually I met my younger brother, who was too young to form a real relationship with me then. But years later, bonding over a shared disappointment with our father, we'd become as close as two siblings raised under the same roof.

On the occasional weekend, Conrad—my father—took Jasen and me to his relatives' houses in Brooklyn. These were his aunts and uncles from St. Thomas, who kept to their old ways and welcomed me with open arms, insisting on feeding me dishes they had learned to make in the Islands. The way they doted on me made it obvious that they felt bad about my father's abandoning me. One aunt was a foster mother, always with a house full of other people's children. I also learned the difference between nature and nurture, since my father was basically a stranger and yet we were so much alike: witty, dry, guarded, self-aware, unapologetic. Whenever I called my father at his corporate office, his first question was not one of worry, warmth, or concern, but suspicion.

"Why are you calling?" he'd ask. "What are you calling for?" he'd press.

"I'm just calling to say hello," I'd insist.

"Because I don't have any money," he always lied.

"That's not why I'm calling." My voice would betray my annoyance.

The truth was, it was often money that made me call my father. If we didn't have enough food or I needed a new pair of shoes, I'd call in the hope that he would care enough to offer his help without my asking, but he never did. At that time, the government had not yet initiated any helpful program forcing deadbeat dads to pay so that their children could live on more than love and fresh air, a little above the poverty line. My father was willing to be in my life in a limited way as long as I didn't ask him to help feed and clothe me. He stated in plain English his unwillingness to contribute to my well-being, so if I wanted to talk that would be fine, but I should have no expectations of placing my hand in his pockets. As I got to know my father I would argue with him about his lack of financial contribution, to which he would always respond, "Life is not fair, Stephanie." There was no comeback capable of guilting him or changing his belief that we, even me, his child, should always be responsible for ourselves. The irony was that my father grew up with servants, a boy who never wanted for anything.

I also learned that Cecilia's godmother, Gerda, was actually my father's only sibling. I started spending the weekends with my aunt and her daughters, Dorie, who was one year younger, and Lisa, six months older than me. My aunt was as tough as my mother, career driven, with real ideas of how children were supposed to behave. She was a dean at Pace University and attended Columbia University at night. Her father, my paternal grandfather, also graduated from Columbia, worked as a professor at Hunter College, and wrote textbooks.

I found it interesting to meet my white-collar family, who lived a completely different reality than my mother's side. While my mother's family had been predominantly blue collar, my father's side had mostly received secondary degrees from Ivy League universities. The more time I spent with my aunt, who resembles me much more than my mother, the more I became like my aunt. They had been friends as teenagers, but I could sense my mother's resentment of my aunt sweeping in after almost thirteen years of silence and showing me a better life and a brighter future. Lisa and I loved having a new cousin and got along great. Dorie had a slight learning disability, but my aunt insisted that at twelve she learn how to travel door to door on weekends from her boarding school in upstate New York. My aunt believed we were capable of anything and didn't stand for our belief in limitations, always forcing us to raise our expectations of ourselves.

Years later I would discover that when my mother first told my father she was pregnant, he went to his mother, who promptly convinced him to escape the situation by joining the service. After my father was released from the army, he returned home and married. Eventually, my mother learned that he was stateside, and she took him to court to wrangle some child support out of him. If he was not willing to be responsible, then the courts would force him. My mother sat in the courtroom listening as my father and his mother testified that I could not possibly be his child. Well, of course the judge denied the claim and allowed my father to shirk his responsibilities. If this happened today, DNA would have slapped the reality across his face and woken him up, but this was long before modern science had made Jerry Springer and Montel Williams famous for "Are you the daddy?" episodes of their talk shows.

And so I learned to accept that the father in my fantasy was nothing like the one I was related to in flesh and blood. As I got older I was able to argue and fight with him, but rarely would I get any emotional reaction from him. My mother and father were realistic to a fault when it came to the harshest truths about life. Neither of them were emotional creatures, instead seeing life from a serious vantage point. They were both incapable of providing emotional sustenance to a scared child, instead painting the picture exactly as it was, which is not what I needed from them.

Missing Mommy

It was shortly after I met my sperm donor that my mother suffered a nervous breakdown or, as the older women in my family called it, "a need for some quiet time." I'm sure a good therapist might find cause to tie the two events together, however loosely, but my mother had been dangling precariously on a very short rope for a long time. I was in Junior High School 35 when my aunt Susie picked me up from school with news that my mother had taken ill.

My family always tried to dispense information to children on a need-to-know basis, and they never believed we needed to know about breakdowns and suicide attempts. Of course, the Covingtons had notoriously big mouths, and before long the real reason my mother was in the hospital trickled down to me.

My childhood had already been marred by one of those "harmless" spilled Covington secrets that I definitely would have been better off not knowing when a well-intentioned cousin told me about my mother's reaction upon discovering she was pregnant with me—her third child—by a third boyfriend. Barely twenty, my mother had scraped together some money and, along with her cousin, traveled to the Lower East Side of Manhattan to a backstreet abortionist. My mother's feet were strongly held in the stirrups as the doctor pushed her back onto the table. But although she knew she didn't have enough money or love to offer another child, she somehow found the strength to get up from the table and go home before the doctor could perform the operation. My mother was not sure if the Catholic orphanage that had raised her colored her decision, but she knew she couldn't have an abortion. And while she hoped that this boyfriend would stay (unlike the last two sperm donors) and truly father this child, she also felt she didn't have a choice.

For the two months my mother was hospitalized for her breakdown, I lived in the Dean Street Projects with Aunt Susie, Uncle Sonny, Deborah, Felicia, and Daniel while Renee lived with my uncle John in Queens, and Cecilia stayed with our grandmother in the Fort Green Projects. I wasn't worried about Renee; she was nobody's victim and even told me later that my uncle had offered her money for sex, which she turned down, threatening to expose him and telling him never to proposition her again.

Even though my mother was not comfortable expressing her feelings, I knew she loved me, and I felt her absence. At home, we'd spend an hour or so a couple nights a week sitting together and watching *M*A*S*H*, *Maude*, *Barney Miller*, or other favorite TV shows before retiring to our separate rooms. My sisters always stayed in their rooms—those nights were a time for just me and my mother, and now she was gone. I hadn't realized how much I depended on her arrival from work in the evening, the sound of her key in the door, and the comfort it brought to me. I also was not used to sharing a room and not having space to be by myself. I had come to embrace the solitude, where I didn't have to pretend to be happy or a part of a family, and now every moment of every day was spent with other people. I had nowhere to go to escape into the fantasy world I preferred, because every room held a body or two.

In my own way, I was a momma's girl, and now she was gone, and I became lost. I played it cool, acting as if things were normal, but inside I just hoped my mom would return home safely.

My aunt took me to Manhattan to visit my mom in the hospital; this was before I came to understand that Bellevue was synonymous with crazy people. Seeing her rendered helpless in that hospital bed scared me. My mother the almighty had loomed larger than life, a giant among the mere mortals in my family, while this woman in the hospital bed, medicated on pills, pretending we weren't in this facility and that everything was normal, was a stranger. My aunt Susie, eagle-eyed and protective of her cubs, dropped my hand, nudging me toward my mother. I approached, fighting back tears, and let her grab my hand. I climbed up on the bed next to her, trying to comfort her when all I wanted was to snatch the covers off and take her back home, where she and I belonged. It would be later in the bathroom of my aunt's apartment—the only available spot for solitude in her kid-filled home—when I broke down and cried for my mother, for my sisters, and for myself. I was older than when I'd become a ward of the state, and my aunt was family and not a stranger, but I knew what it was like to feel displaced.

The two things I did like about living with my aunt were Felicia's clothes—which we shared and which were much nicer than my own—and the food. My aunt was a good cook, and food was always plentiful in her house. Afternoon snacks and full-course dinners were a daily occurrence, no longer a rarity, but the food did not fill me up in the way that I expected.

"Stephanie, slow down," my aunt warned when I'd jump up to get seconds. "The food isn't going anyplace."

But they didn't know what a luxury the meals were for me. I would sneak food into my bed at night, clutching cookies and potato chips like a child's blankie, expecting it to soothe me to sleep. My aunt also gave us money for snacks at school, slipping us change or a dollar here and there on the regular. I would have lived in the projects forever if it meant having tasty food and money for extras. I still remembered my excitement the one time my mother sent me to the store for an Entenmann's coffee cake. Man, that was living.

When my mother was released from the hospital, my relief was short-lived, because she immediately informed the three of us that we would be moving in six months to Norfolk, Virginia. As far as she was concerned, the lack of air and space in the city—not her choice of the wrong men—were the biggest contributors to her breakdown. She had borne the children of three men who failed to love her or us, their daughters. And I later learned that during those weekends and summers spent with my relatives, my mother had had additional relationships, her most recent with a married man who had lied about loving her. Well, one more disappointment piled onto a lifetime of disappointment had sent my mother over the edge and straight into the loony bin, and now she decided that a geographic change was the answer to her problems. I returned home from my aunt's house to find my mother already packing up our apartment.

Two summers before, my grandmother had bravely hauled us grandchildren to Norfolk to visit her deceased brother's family. That trip had been my introduction not only to the South but to the tradition of removing a heavy tree branch, called a switch, for your own beating. But my mother had never even been to Virginia, and here she had committed to living there based on my grandmother's word. Since my mother generally scoffed at everything my grandmother said or suggested, I could not understand why we were moving hundreds of miles away on her say-so.

"There is no damn air in this city," she explained to anyone who dared to question her choice.

Less than a month later, my mother had packed up our tenement and moved everything into storage. My aunt Hattie, a close family friend, had left her two-bedroom doorman building in our care while she and her son, Clean, left the country for work. My mother continued to earn, barely spending any money as she saved up for our Southern future.

A month before my graduation from JHS 35, my mother took off for Norfolk, leaving me once again with my aunt Susie. My father volunteered or was coerced or badgered into taking me to Bloomingdale's for my graduation outfit, a first. I'm sure the danger of my mother having a permanent break from reality and his being forced to take responsibility for my daily care and feeding caused him to momentarily get a conscience.

I felt so grown up on Graduation Day, especially since my father did not know that the high heels and tight skirt he purchased would have never been approved by my mother. The graduation celebration culminated at Junior's Cheesecake in downtown Brooklyn, a neighborhood staple specializing in some of the best cheesecake on the East Coast. True to her word, Renee stayed with Uncle John in Queens. Immediately afterward, I packed the rest of my belongings and, along with a pissed-off Cecilia, took the Greyhound bus to Norfolk to be reunited with our mother.

A Communist
Among Us

My mother met us at the bus station, driving a burgundy 1966 T-Bird. Unbeknownst to us, she had recently learned to drive. The moment we climbed in, her novice maneuvers struck terror in us girls.

We remained silent as she grilled us on the events of the past months. Our relatives did not believe in wasting hard-earned money on long-distance phone calls, so we had to depend on the mulelike service of the U.S. postal workers. Although my mother always had a way with words, those words rarely found their way to a mailbox. She did write letters, but only occasionally did she mail them, and when they were received the information was outdated.

It was unusual that she had managed to keep her driving a secret from us, what with her being a Covington, which made her automatically unable to hold water. Maybe she knew that neither of us would have boarded the bus at the Port Authority if we had known in advance that at the other end of our twelve-hour journey she was waiting behind the wheel. Her passing a driving test and being given a license to put two innocent girls' lives in jeopardy should have been against a law somewhere on the books. On the terrifying drive to our new home in Norfolk, a suburb of trees and one-story buildings, we did all we could to keep from screaming. The slightest noise could shift our mother's mood irreparably, and we were unwilling to take the risk.

The downtown area where the bus arrived reminded me of those small towns in old western movies. You know, the sleepy half-dead places waiting for trouble to ride into town to liven things up. I hoped half seriously that we weren't the influx of liveliness this small 'burb needed to awaken.

To say it was culture shock would downplay the impact. By the time we arrived at our new address, a one-story brick duplex in a neighborhood where nothing grew taller than a two-story building, I could have been Dorothy and this might as well have been Kansas, as far as the foreignness of the landscape. Virginia was an alternate reality, nothing like the crowded hustle and largeness of New York City, and we knew on sight that we hated it. Cecilia began to plot her escape back to civilization while I tried to appease my mother with bubbly tales, lying about my happiness and excitement at this new adventure.

My all-black inner-city school, covered in graffiti, littered with torn pages from textbooks, was replaced by a large, pristine building on a manicured lawn, teeming with both well-heeled preppy kids and country kids. They were all one big happy family and, like any extended family, different factions splintered off without any complaint or hostility from the others. Everyone coexisted with an unspoken agreement of interdependence, as if there were a dozen schools functioning under one large roof. Unlike all my other moves, where I dived into the role of class clown, guaranteeing a speedy boost in popularity, this time I stayed invisible and avoided making friends, because I became convinced of the temporariness of the situation. All the other times we moved, I still lived close enough to Felicia to spend my weekends with her. As different as our neighborhoods in Brooklyn could be, there was always a familiar stench of poverty that felt like home, and this seemed like Mars.

I spent all my free time after school at the local library, often returning home at night after it closed. Had this been New York my mother would have denied me the freedom to explore the real world, but she considered Virginia a safe place where the danger she feared all her life would never appear from around a corner. The bedroom community lulled her into a false sense of contentment, and she forgot that there were other things more dangerous than strangers, like feelings of abandonment and displacement. I retreated into myself, making the local library my safety net. I could always find comfort in the stacks of books offering me the vantage point of a different world where dreams came true and happy endings did in fact exist.

Another thing that added to my discomfort was my mother's involvement in the Workers World Party, the Communist movement. My mother, who had always bemoaned the inequities of life, had finally found a forum to rage against the unjust system that was America. She didn't see the world in terms of black and white but rich and poor. My mother believed we were living under a harsh dictator since we fell on the lowest rung of the invisible caste system. So she chose to dedicate her attention to those whose slippery hands and broken beliefs made it difficult to climb to even that bottom rung. It didn't seem to faze her that among those who suffered injustice and poverty and whose needs were not met were her children, who suddenly found themselves alone in an alternate universe with a stranger for a mother.

My mother's sudden increased interest in activism was foreshadowed early on by the rent strikes she organized in our buildings whenever a slumlord refused to repair a broken-down tenement. She constantly forced the slumlord to fix up the building by refusing to pay rent and organizing the tenants to follow her example. Each time she dragged the landlord off to court we faced possible eviction, but my mother, armed with at least a few troublemaker tenants and their stack of Polaroids documenting the physical evidence of unlivable conditions, always won her case. Had she been afforded an adequate education, my mother would have made an exemplary defense attorney championing the underdogs. Even with her limited power she loved to right the wrongs of the world, but I still had no idea how this desire would affect my life.

Any belief I had in being rescued into normalcy vanished when my mother fell in love with a younger white man who wore a Santa Claus beard. Bob was at the forefront of the movement, spending his postcollege years rebelling against his doctor father and his society mother, who sat on the board of local charities along with the museum. In our former life in Brooklyn the blacks and whites were happily separated, living in different neighborhoods, attending different schools, shopping in different stores, and made no pains or attempts at interaction. Everything about my pre-Virginia world was chocolate; at school the teachers, hyped up on Black Power, taught African American history, wore blown-out afros and dashikis, and called us "young brother" and "young sister." They made a point to teach us to be proud of our blackness, telling us we were the chosen ones and that being black was a privilege, but mostly that Black was Beautiful. Kids at school wore Afro picks with a carved fist as the handle in their hair, and red, black, and green were the colors of the flag that we waved in celebration of our ancestors. At school assembly we sang the Negro anthem, "To Be Young, Gifted, and Black," and we believed that we were. It wasn't about being president or hating whiteness, but we finally had the validation we needed to transcend our battered roots of slavery. So this transition into a vanilla-filled world didn't sit well with me or Cecilia. We had learned about our forty acres and a mule, and we knew reverse migration was not the way to claim our inheritance. But my mother, who had never found a black man to stay and love her in the way that she needed, found something in Bob. Years later my friend and I would joke, "Once you go black you never go back," and it always made me think of my mother.

Bob did his best to get his parents' attention by falling in love with a black mother of three, eight years his senior. Before long my mother was spending all her free time with her comrades in the movement, or party, as it was known to insiders, rarely coming home before nine or ten at night. When she did return home, Bob smooshed beside her, she failed to take any interest in her life outside the party. If Cecilia and I refused to go to meetings with her, she called us selfish and couldn't understand where she had gone wrong. She considered us to be extensions of her, so she assumed we'd feel the same passion that she did. Neither of us knew how to navigate this minefield of newness, mostly because we didn't want to. So even if we couldn't rebel out loud for fear of our mother, we retreated from her and these new interests, letting our indifference do the talking. When she came home we'd hide out in our room, refusing to befriend her, Bob, or this new world we'd been dropped into.

One night my mother and Bob took us to a restaurant, hoping to bond. In my extended family most wars were settled over food, where collard greens could turn anger into celebration. Cecilia and even I were immune to the temptation of an open menu and were borderline rude. Neither Cecilia nor I accepted this olive branch as my mother and Bob happily chatted about their future, where we were relegated to bit players who should have been thrilled to be included at all. As Bob peppered us with questions and inquiries about our new lives too close to the Mason-Dixon Line, we gave clipped, one-word answers. Unlike all the other times we had been tromped out to play our role of happy children, we refused to pretend for this audience. Across from us, my mother's hazel eyes blazed like those of an angry cat about to claw our faces for threatening her happiness, but we were angry, too. Like hungry puppies we had always obeyed our mother, lapping up her orders, fetching her cigarettes, happy for whatever praise or attention she gave us, but this time we had been pushed too far. She had chosen this movement and this man over us, and we were not about to make it all right. My sister and I even threw in some current colloquialisms we'd picked up in Bed-Stuy in order to affirm our blackness to Bob. Of course we incurred our mother's wrath for our disobedience.

She responded to our insubordination by retreating further into this new world. The tension between Cecilia and Bob escalated. Unlike me, who preferred to be invisible, Cecilia refused to hide her dislike for Bob or the backseat we now took to our mother's new interests. She railed at the lack of food or heat or fairness in this new situation. At seventeen she already had one foot out the door and didn't have much patience or interest in keeping the peace. As the first grandchild Cecilia had always been the chosen one. She knew that crying on our grandmother's shoulder guaranteed her passage back to the Big Apple, and she took it, returning to New York to live in the Fort Green Projects with our grandmother.

Without any real warning I became an only child, alone with my mother and her boyfriend in this new and unappealing world. By this time my mother had moved us into lower-income housing inhabited mostly by naval families. Even though my mother rallied against the government, she'd put us in an environment where we were surrounded by government employees. I was a nonbeliever in a world of believers, like walking into a church waving a banner stating that you are a practicing atheist.

I befriended our next-door neighbors, an all-blond naval family, Jeff, Pam, and their daughter, Jill. Jill, age four, became my closest friend, and she and her parents became my surrogate family. They were in their early twenties, smoked pot, loved rock and roll, and fed me nightly while my mother marched off fighting the inequities of the world. Eventually Bob moved in with us, although my mother swore he had his own apartment, but I saw no proof of that. They were so busy unionizing coal mines, staging rent strikes, and fighting to right other real or imagined wrongs in the world that they became a blur.

I kept to myself for the most part, reading books that were further removed from this new reality. I became a Harlequin Romance junkie, seeking pure fantasy and escapism.

My mother insisted it was my civic duty to contribute to the movement regardless of how responsible I believed the party was in forcing me to raise myself. As far as she was concerned I had to become her clone whether I liked it or not. With Cecilia gone, I didn't have the courage to stand up to my mother, no matter how much I hated being around her new friends. She saw my inclusion as an opportunity for us to spend precious bonding time, but I saw it as a dictatorship similar to that of Stalin, her idol. The room was filled with comrades, mainly social outcasts of one kind or another: ex–flower children, vets, rebelling WASPs and lay Catholics, and others pissed off at their families and the current administration.

The one thing I understood quickly was that none of these people had grown up in a crappy tenement where their basic needs went unmet. Real poor people are too busy worrying about the next paycheck, next job, next meal, rent, bills, and on and on, to care what the government is doing.

I doubted any one person in that room had ever been popular, and while the pursuit of popularity would seem absurd to this group, at thirteen it became my obsession. Since it was clear to me that for the moment New York was not an option, I had begun to make friends and find my way, meeting lots of urban kids who had been banished to the South to live with grandparents and other family members. Again, my survival instinct kicked into full gear, so I chose peers whose refrigerators were full and whose mothers stayed at home, delighted to provide sustenance for a well-mannered friend of their children. At school I tried to blend, hoping no one would get a glimpse of the horror that was my household. High school is already a hormonal nightmare, with everyone jockeying for top dog, so I wanted to be seen as just another normal kid and not the freak who lived with her strange mother and white hippie boyfriend in a place often filled to overflowing with weirdos and castoffs. This school was not the place to stand out from the crowd unless you were ubercool or exceptional in some area, which I wasn't. Luckily for him, the one Hispanic kid in school was a star athlete, making him popular among both races. This was the late 1970s, and very few blacks and whites mixed in the South in those days, so I was afraid to be perceived as someone different. Though this was postsegregation, the two races preferred to keep their personal lives separate, and truthfully I could not have agreed more with this arrangement.

My mother, always quick to wrest me from the jaws of happiness, demanded I join her in saving the underdogs of the world and on the weekends forced me to hand out flyers alongside her comrades at the local parks, where my schoolmates gathered to have fun. Other than my mother, I only ever saw two black people in the party: Monica Moorehead and her boyfriend John. We also spent lots of time picketing naval bases, Norfolk's main source of income being the military. If I ever spoke out against the movement, I had no chance—my mother's newfound knowledge fought off even the staunchest disbeliever. To her the movement offered an alternative to the passive, victimized life of her past, and she took to the power, however limited, like a hungry dog to a bone. Whenever the movement staged a rally out of town, I was dragged along against my will. At one point, we were marching on Washington so often it would have been easier to live there.

The only positive part about going on marches was the food. I looked forward to the massive number of child-free comrades willing to feed me. I was the only teenager in a movement full of adults who believed the world too crowded to procreate and who took pleasure in taking me to lunch and trying to become my friend. They wanted to know what I thought of the world, how my generation saw things, and if I was as passionate as my mother about making change happen. Rather than shout a loud *Hell no*, I couldn't risk losing my meal tickets, so I played along.

Out of the watchful eye of my mother I grew animated, revealing parts of myself I would have never exposed to my own parent. These people didn't need me to be anything or to think anything; they just seemed to want to know who I was and what I believed. On the marches I could trick two or three different people to feed me; like a squirrel storing away nuts for the future I ate as many large meals as I was offered. Newly thirteen, I found myself marching in front of the White House holding a large banner demonstrating for gay rights. Rights, gay or otherwise, were actually not on my radar, but I knew that by participating I would be rewarded with food and dessert and people who were genuinely interested in me being myself instead of me having to be a mini version of my mother.

The ERA (Equal Rights Amendment for women) movement lasted the longest, with rallies being held in major cities every weekend for almost a year. My mother raged against my apathy over political activism, which she believed would improve my life. She ranted about women's rights while the smell of liver and onions mingled with the cigarette-filled air in our house and made it impossible to breathe, so forget about me hearing her. My goal was more in alignment with punishing my mother for her absence, not rewarding her with my presence. I hated the movement, hated my mother's involvement in it, and would have given anything to return to a roach-infested tenement back in Brooklyn, which had become my Holy Grail.

My mother didn't do anything halfway. Eventually she left her secretarial job in favor of a part-time position that gave her more time for the movement. The party offered my mother a voice, a chance to be vocal about all the injustices she had suffered at the hands of others and more.

My mother and Bob purchased a puke-green house on Lyons Avenue, a middle-class black-and-white neighborhood. It was a run-down two-story monstrosity on a double plot of land, the eyesore of the block. My mother's rural fantasy played out in the garden she insisted on growing on the side of that rambling house.

Food at home also got worse around this time. My mother and Bob believed food to be an unnecessary luxury and chose to live on fried liver and onions. I hated liver and took to eating at friends' houses or going to bed hungry in protest. Sometimes I could tell that they had eaten out at a restaurant before returning home, or they'd boldly enter with leftover soft drinks from a fast-food place. My mother invited me to meetings, dangling the luxury of dinner as long as I went to the meetings with them. Unless I was starving I'd figure out a plan B instead of sitting through hours of Communist rantings. For Christ's sake, I wasn't a Communist or a Republican or a Democrat or even a liberal; I was a teenager, and that's all I wanted to be.

Usually after school I'd scrounge through Bob's and my mother's pockets and come up with enough change to buy a couple of potatoes to make French fries. We also had a pecan tree in the backyard, and if I could gather enough money for a stick of butter I would bake pecan-butter cookies, which were delicious.

Luckily I spent many weekends with my aunt Ethellee and cousin Greg or my second cousins Nita and Beverly. Both of these homes afforded the comfort of stability and food. My aunts would cook hearty breakfasts and always made sure I had enough to eat. To them food was love, which they lavished on me in unlimited portions. These women took great pride in feeding their families substantial Southern meals. On Sundays they made feasts that rivaled Thanksgiving. These meals took days to prepare, but they rarely complained about all the hard work. In order to be a part of this Sunday dinner ritual I would have to attend church. There was no way I could show up on their doorstep on Sunday afternoon expecting a vibrant welcome. It's not that I would be turned away, but I'd be reminded (loudly) that Sunday was the Lord's day and I needed to go to church to give thanks before partaking in his abundance. I knew better than to admit to my atheist Communist mother that I happily went to church with my cousins, excited about the meal that would follow. She did find out from our choir director cousin that I got tossed out of the choir for being tone deaf, something she shares. I think she was just relieved that I had found something I liked about Virginia, so she let me spend most weekends with my family.

I began to make friends and settle into this unnatural life. My best friends, Zondra and Berthel, and I went bike riding after school, stopping at the basketball court where they distracted their boyfriends from sports with heavy petting sessions. At thirteen I still had more interest in Barbie than boys. Zondra joined me on marches with my mother and Bob, her skeptical parents allowing her cries to sway them into letting her go. Zondra was a daddy's girl, something I knew nothing about, and she could convince her father to let her do most things even when her mother disagreed.

In September I began my sophomore year at Maury High School, ignorant of the fact that my mother would soon find a way to invade my one island of normality. She left her part-time job, chucking fashionable suits, pantyhose, and makeup for overalls, plaid shirts, and Timberlands. This is at a time when women, especially in the South, dressed like women and were easily identifiable. My mother's unisex outfits made her stand out as a rebel in a world of conformists, and the glare of that eventually shone a spotlight onto me whether I liked it or not. She took a job driving the bright yellow school bus to my high school, which seemed like the cruelest of all jokes. But to my mother this was simply another way to be involved in my life and to show that she was interested in my world. She didn't care how her new job embarrassed me, insisting it was for my benefit so that we could spend quality time together. How my mother managed to hold on to her driver's license was still a mystery, so I couldn't believe anyone would allow her to helm a bus loaded with other people's children. If I had some residual fantasy of being popular, the daily vision of my mother tromping past my locker dressed like a lumberjack killed my last hopes of transforming into the school's "it" girl. I refused to believe it had anything to do with the fact that at fourteen I still lacked breasts, my monthly period, or any signs of impending womanhood. Even though I hadn't yet peaked in high school I had a lot of friends, navigating between the jocks, nerds, drama class, cheerleaders, popular kids, the hip black kids from the hood, and those in my neighborhood. I had friends among all the cliques but never joined any one group; instead I circulated equally, keeping my distance from all of them. I was superfriendly with a wicked sense of humor and a little bit of knowledge about most things, which added to my popularity.

As much as my mother tried to smash Bob and me together, sending us on runs to the store, it was obvious he and I would never be more than forced acquaintances. Bob's age rested almost equally between my mother's and mine. I resented his presence in our lives, and the feeling was mutual, but for my mother's sake we pretended to get along. He would have preferred his relationship with my mother to come with only one mouth to feed and nobody issuing him dirty looks and long disapproving silences. I knew that as much as he liked my mother, he wasn't committed to sharing the burden of her children, and before long he gave up any pretenses otherwise. If he knew my mother was coming home late, he ate elsewhere, ignoring our bare refrigerator because after all I wasn't his kid. I can't say he took pleasure in my hunger, but he refused to take responsibility for my meals. When rallies were taking place in our town I slept over at friends' houses, only to come home to strange white people lying in every available space in my bedroom.

One Sunday I returned home to find a "Free the Wilmington Ten" gathering. The Wilmington Ten, nine young white men and one white woman, were charged with arson of a white-owned grocery store and conspiracy. The comrades were incensed by the injustices these young people were receiving for crimes no one believed they had committed. Even after the witnesses recanted their testimonies and one admitted to receiving a bike in exchange for his testimony, the Ten were still convicted. Seated among the group of radicals in my house that day was the Reverend Benjamin Chavis Sr., father of the Reverend Ben Chavis Jr., one of the Ten and a man who would eventually helm the NAACP. Chavis Sr., who stayed with us while in town for the rally, was a kind, soft-spoken, dignified man who I'm sure believed this wild bunch of Communist rebels was insane. Because of his love for his son, he took the help where he could get it, and the party was not afraid to use their loud voices to help free the Ten.

At school I asserted my normalcy by joining the drama club and feigning interest in the Young Republicans. I rebelled by seeking out the quiet Right to my mother's loud Left. Somehow, though, even as I was denying the validity of the Workers World Party, it began to have an effect on how I saw the world. It became harder to be a passive participant when I didn't agree with something.

One morning as the class recited the Pledge of Allegiance, I began to question the practice. At first calmly and rationally, but then before I could contain myself, I became all shades of my mother: loud, fiery, and convinced I was right. My homeroom teacher, not used to disobedience, demanded I join the rest of the class in the Pledge.

"What if I don't believe that 'liberty and justice for all' is true? It's not like that in America. At least not my America," I insisted.

"Stephanie, say the Pledge or you will get sent to the principal's office," she explained, and that's when it all turned.

"I'm not saying something I don't believe. You want me to lie?" I asked.

She was fuming. "Say the Pledge or you're going to the principal's office."

"Fuck the Pledge, I'm not saying it." I rolled my eyes and was done.

Sitting in the principal's office waiting for my mother, I knew I was about to get a smackdown. Although my mother cursed like a sailor (I certainly didn't learn to curse in the streets like some of my friends—I got my lessons at home) and had little respect for authority herself, disrespecting an adult rated serious trouble in her book. The whole ride home she lectured me on respecting adults. Here I expected her to be proud of me. I did the very thing she wanted—I had questioned authority. I had fought the system the way she had been teaching me my whole life. I stood up to something I didn't believe in, and now I was in trouble.

On our ride home, I flashed back to third grade, when my mother had taken me out of public school and put me in Catholic school. The entire year was about me fighting the battles she had been unable to fight as a helpless young girl left in the care of the Catholic Church. While the dress code strictly enforced dark green plaid uniform skirts and dresses for girls, my mother regularly sent me to school in pants: "You tell them your mother said it was all you had." Chapel became another of her battles: "You tell those nuns to prove to you God exists." She'd make me question them, ensuring I'd be seen as class freak. I became known as the troublemaker among the good Catholic girls. And now she was insisting I be punished for cursing, questioning.

"Don't think these three days are gonna be some vacation," she hissed.

For my entire suspension I pulled weeds out of her burgeoning garden. I hated that garden, and once my punishment was over, I never went near it again, no matter how many times she tried to encourage me. We were not the Joads and this was not *Grapes of Wrath* and I wanted no part of her rural fantasy.

Gradually I was coming to see my current mother as a stranger, separate from and different than my mother before her breakdown. Breakdown Mom had swallowed my mom whole. Prebreakdown Mom was quite cool and regular compared with this loud, brash comrade who didn't care what she looked like.

Around this time, once again, food became a missing component in my already unhappy life. When my mother was home, I could usually depend on her to remember she had to feed me, even if it was liver and onions. But then Renee and her best friend Michelle moved in with us. Renee needed a change, since her high school sweetheart had been arrested for robbing a store, getting eight years for armed robbery at age fourteen.

Once Renee and Michelle, two headstrong, opinionated, sixteen-year-old New Yorkers, saw how I had been neglected with the sporadic food supply, they protested by refusing to show manners to my mother or to give Bob any respect. Resentment between Bob and Renee and Michelle grew when he began to purchase dinner solely for him and my mother. My mother, angry at the girls for causing friction in her relationship, refused to get involved and kept silent. I, of course, was blackballed alongside the other girls. They spoke out against me being compelled to participate in rallies, and for a while I wasn't forced to be the youngest Communist. My mother didn't want to explain to her comrades why three girls, voices of tomorrow, could not be swayed to stand up for their causes. Weekly checks from Michelle's mother, along with help from extended family, kept us fed. Unlike in New York, where we felt an allegiance to our mother, we became vocal about life inside the house and the disparity between my mother and Bob and us. He always had money for marijuana but would not feed us.

But before long, Renee and Michelle returned to New York and a life of nourishment and fun, and life in Virginia returned to what it was before; again I was left alone to fend for myself and was forced along on protest marches. When not eating out, my mother and Bob continued the diet of liver and onions whenever I was around, a food I still to this day cannot stand to smell.

My relief came in the form of Felicia and Deborah. Felicia and I could not stand to be apart, and after our crying and whining, our mothers relented, and my cousins came to live with us. My aunt Susie never let her kids go hungry, and she sent food stamps and cash on a regular basis to ensure we would eat. But my aunt didn't understand her sister, one year older than she, living in a falling-down house with a hairy white man and with little interest in nurturing her own children. My mother took the childhood she had never been given and lived it all these years later. Her involvement in the movement grew deeper and more committed. Before long the stories of her neglect and Bob's meanness reached back to New York, and my aunt Susie collected her children, giving a "let me tell you about yourself" tongue lashing to my mother before she left in a huff.

The Workers World Party gave my mother the thing that had always been absent in her life, community and a sense of belonging. It validated her in ways motherhood never had. It allowed her, who had always been a victim, to finally have a voice, and if she lost her children in the process it was preferable to losing herself again. She had found her chance to fit in somewhere, and she was not about to relinquish it. She had been raised without a voice—a poor black woman didn't have a huge chance in the world of her past and now she was passionate that others would never feel as powerless and alone. And I swear, as much as I hate to admit it, she came alive before my eyes. I remember it was at the time that my mother sat me down and explained her reasoning for choosing the party over me. Of course she would have never phrased it that way. She saw the party as a way to give me the future that I deserved.

"You are poor, you're black, and you're a woman. You started this life with three strikes against you, and it is my job to change those odds. I need to make this world a place of equality for you and your sisters. Do you understand?" she pleaded.

She wanted me to assuage her guilt at being absent from my needs. It was one thing to understand and another to feel OK with something.

"Mom, it's fine," I promised, giving her permission to further abandon me.

I knew that nothing I said would change the path she had put herself on, and no matter how I felt, I didn't want to burden my mother by needing her. So I stayed silent. I spent time with friends and family, but mainly I stayed in my bedroom away from Bob and my mother, when they were around. Occasionally my mother went on trips and left me alone with Bob. Usually I stayed with my aunt Ethellee and my cousin Greg, but sometimes if it was only a day and I had school, she'd leave me home.

I found myself starving alternately for affection and for food until it became impossible to separate the two. I continued to choose my friendships based on the fullness of refrigerators and the presence of attentive, doting mothers. I slipped further into survival mode by stealing some of Bob's pot and giving it to a stoner classmate who sold it and split the profits with me. Finally, I had my own money and no longer had to attend my mother's meetings in order to eat. As hungry as I was for food, my real hunger was for my mother. She didn't seem to mind if I ate or if every afternoon my girlfriends and I spent time with horny men-children trying to steal our innocence. My mother preferred running off to Pennsylvania to unionize coal mines or to Baltimore to help rent strikes, and nothing I did helped me win back her attention.

The Trouble
with Puberty

The most dramatic step I took to separate myself from my mother was to become a cheerleader, a bubbly female mascot, second banana to the more important male athletes. I might as well have hung a sign around my neck announcing that I was a traitor to the female gender. Passing the Equal Rights Amendment was the cornerstone of my mother's political agenda, so this was a huge slap in her face. To my mother, feminism was not an option; it was the only choice if you were a self-respecting woman, and my decision told her I wasn't.

My mother looked at me as if she were seeing me for the first time: this person quivering slightly in front of her was not the daughter she had raised but a stranger. And she was not happy.

I determined at that moment that no matter what she said or did I would not back down and lose my chance at normalcy and popularity, typical twin desires at age fifteen. She lectured me that the one reason she had joined the party was to ensure that her girls had better options than she'd had. I refused to be swayed from my position by any of her tactics. The harder she tried, the more my demeanor shifted from that of a scared kid to that of a truly determined teenager.

And she hit the roof. "No daughter of mine is going to be a cheerleader. Not in this lifetime."

I did not respond; I rejoiced quietly at her threats.

"Do you have any idea what you are saying to the world?" she demanded.

"Uh—that I want to be popular?" I threw the words out there, knowing they couldn't possibly be the answer she sought, smart-ass enough to earn me a smack.

She had no idea of the magnitude of the good fortune that had befallen me, and I was not about to squander it. I wanted this too much. I saw the status of cheerleader as a way to vault from the invisible back row of high school to front and center. The gift of acceptance being dangled before me meant so much—too much for me to give up.

So as my mother raged on about her disappointment at my being corrupted by the system, the torrent fell on deaf ears; I was mentally preparing for my new elevated station in life. Finally, I would have a seat at the popular table, and all my problems would be over. Such was the seductive power of fame for the naive.

My change in status had come about that past week. Three cheerleaders, Peaches—my friend and a sister to one of the cheerleaders—and I had started our Monday morning having cocktails in the girls' bathroom. I'd never done anything like that before, but they invited me, and just like so many girls that age I said yes to drinking because I wanted them to like me. An invitation to hang with three girls whose social status at school was legendary was too big an opportunity to pass up. I'm not saying I would have followed them off a building, but I probably would have checked to see how far the fall would be.

But Mrs. White, the cheerleading coach—Barbie married to a Ken-doll husband, Mr. White, the basketball coach—

heard the boisterous, drunken conversation through the adjoining female teachers' bathroom, and we could hear her shouting at us. I shook with terror. This time it would not be another mild suspension—it would make my last punishment of weed pulling pale in comparison. This was real trouble.

Recognizing the three voices of her cheerleaders, Mrs. White called them out into the hall by name, where the stench of alcohol sent them immediately to the principal's office and into suspension, hence three openings magically appeared on the squad. It was sheer luck that she didn't enter the bathroom and find me and Peaches. The girls were tossed out of school for an indefinite period, so I knew they wouldn't brand me a traitor for suddenly rocking their old cheerleading uniform.

Now that the cool girls were gone from the squad, the appeal of being a cheerleader lost its luster among the more talented, popular girls. One slot easily became mine, and another went to Peaches. No way could my mother keep me from joining the squad.

Of course she believed otherwise. "I am not giving you the money for a uniform," she announced triumphantly.

But I had a better hand and played it. "My father is sending me the money," I told her with all the smugness of a teenager who doesn't understand the pain of the arrow she has just slung.

Having my father give me cash for the frivolous activity of cheerleading when money for food and bills was sparse pissed off my mother. For the past year she had waged a campaign to get my father to take some financial responsibility for me. She had been writing long, pained letters of teenage angst as though she were me, explaining to my father how much his input, both financial and emotional, were necessary for my self-esteem. (And this was before studies linking a girl's self-esteem to her father's involvement in her life were widely available.) She wrote these letters in her perfect penmanship, then instructed me to copy them in my flawed adolescent handwriting. I was too young and self-involved to understand the desperation my mother must have felt to use this tactic to loosen my father's grip on his money. All I knew was that I hated writing such personal details of my life to him, especially since they were my mother's version of my life, not my own.

My mother spun these stories as if she had a clue what it felt like to be me. She clearly thought we were the same person inhabiting two bodies, but we weren't. That supertight sitcom mother-daughter bond did not exist between us. In many ways, each of us hoped the other would finally twist herself into our individual ideal so we wouldn't always be so disappointed. My mother was always painting me with the same brushstrokes she used to paint herself, sometimes literally, like the time she decided to dye my hair to match hers one week before I was to start junior high school. She had recently gotten happy with a Clairol bottle and transformed her own locks from an acceptable shade of brown to a bright red Lucille Ball shade. The color didn't look too tragic against my mother's light complexion and hazel eyes, but on a brown-skinned black girl the result was laughable. I raced into the bathroom, my sisters' loud taunts following me, and stared in shock at my reflection in the mirror. There in front of me stood my worst nightmare: nappy hair the color of an orangutan. My mother had destroyed any chance I had to enter junior high school a normal adolescent. To compound matters, my extended family took to calling her "Big Red" and me "Little Red."

My mother no more got "my" communication to my father right than she had my hair. In the letters she had me admitting to him that I was turning sixteen and still had not gotten my period or breasts. What sane sixteen-year-old admits that to her father, especially an unfamiliar one with no personal attachment? None of these manipulation tactics elicited one dime from my father (with the single exception of the cheerleading money), and here I had humiliated myself by asking.

Suddenly my Saturdays were taken up with cheerleading practice instead of marching on picket lines spouting slogans for causes that didn't interest me. The squad raised money doing bake sales and car washes so we could attend cheerleading camp at the College of William and Mary, where there was so much food I almost fainted from happiness. The college cafeteria served buffet style, where every food imaginable presented itself for the taking. I had died and gone to food heaven. I gorged myself at every meal, expecting this treasure trove of sustenance to disappear at any moment. My friends laughed at my gigantic appetite, telling me I had a tapeworm, and at any free moment they knew they'd find me back in the cafeteria. If I went missing, none of my teammates had to figure out where to search for me.

Returning home to an empty fridge when camp was over brought me back to reality. For my mother, food was still about fuel for the body, not about taste or flavor or celebration. It didn't matter what you ate as long as you shoved something in your mouth that gave you the energy to keep going. Another component I had not explored was my mother's chain smoking. There was a real chance that cigarettes had not only destroyed her appetite but also her taste buds, which could have accounted for her lack of interest in food.

In the past we had spent Thanksgiving with our family in New York, but that year we went to the Smalls'—Bob's parents'—house. They lived in a massive home on the banks of a river. To my surprise, the Smalls didn't flinch when we showed up, as if finding a black woman and her illegitimate child seated at their dinner table were the most natural thing. And while they were clearly conservative and traditional, they loved their only son and placed his happiness above any judgments. They went out of their way to make me feel welcome and included, but I desperately missed my family. Thanksgiving dinner at the Smalls' couldn't have been more different than the loud, boisterous Covington holidays I was used to. His mother served turkey, goose liver stuffing, pearl onions, green beans with crunchy onions, salad, and rolls. The bland food lacked the seasonings and taste I had grown up with. It was white people food, but my mother's stern look warned me against my normal tactic of shoving food around the plate. Even the dessert, pumpkin pie instead of sweet potato pie, lacked flavor, but meeting my mother's eyes I knew to eat and shut up about it. The price for embarrassing my mother by acting unmannered was too high for me even during my rebellious phase, so I remained silent, nodded, and issued my pleases and thank-yous.

Fortunately for me, Christmas in New York more than made up for Thanksgiving. As usual, Felicia and I were thick as thieves, and my world felt right side up again. Of the wealth of offspring in my family, we two survived in our own world, sharing not only our aspirations for the future but our fears. She was the one person who could tell by looking at me that something was wrong, which is why she was the only one who knew I had been molested.

She had always been my lifeline and I hers, even though we couldn't have been more different. She was quiet, I was loud; she lacked self-confidence, I pretended to have enough for two; she walked inside the lines, I raged outside the box; she was sweet, I was spicy. But together we were one dynamic, beautiful person.

My grandmother had sixteen grandchildren and would eventually have another twenty-two great-grandchildren. Felicia and I grew up in a world overrun with snotty-nosed, whining kids, and being burdened with a crumb snatcher of my own never appealed to me. But from my earliest memories of Felicia, she craved the chance to be a mother.

"I want a million trillion kids," she would dream aloud to anyone who would listen.

"Not me, I want to travel the world and I want to write about it," I'd respond.

I wanted freedom from being responsible for anyone other than myself. So while Felicia dreamed of a Prince Charming and happily ever after, I was jaded about fairy tales. Nothing in my life allowed me to believe that some man would come and sweep me away to a better life. I had bet on my father rescuing me, and I already explained that disappointment. No, I wanted a future free of fantasy. I wanted to conquer the world by myself, because that way I couldn't get hurt, and no one could abandon me, breaking me into tiny, unrecognizable pieces.

Back in Virginia after the holiday, cheerleading and staying one step away from trouble consumed my time. I discovered that the group of boys in my immediate circle had begun to place bets on my virginity. They each wanted to be the first one to "pop my cherry," my girls confided in me. Zondra insisted, "Girl, it's gonna hurt if you don't do it soon," and others tried to explain to me, "Sex is no big deal." Because my uncle had never been able to fully penetrate me and break my hymen I still considered myself a virgin. Maybe part of the reason I wasn't quick to give up my cherry had to do with the experience of my molestation. I wasn't willing to be manipulated or forced into sex again.

I didn't have any romantic notions about sex and having that first time be with someone I loved. I just couldn't stand how stupid sex seemed to make everybody. Unlike my sisters and girlfriends, I prided myself on not falling for the obvious lies boys told in order to get into my pants. Some were more creative than others, but they were transparent and failed to get me to spread my legs. Having a bet on who popped my cherry made me hold on longer than I even wanted. I wondered why boys worked so hard to steal something they could have gotten more easily by telling the plain truth.

I had recently befriended Reese, the "school slut," as she was called mostly behind her back. Unlike most of my friends who were sleeping with their boyfriends on the sly, Reese made no apologies about her sexual appetite, and the result was the pejorative. When it came to sex, she was like the guys and did it whenever she wanted. If she wanted to have sex with some guy she barely knew, she often made the first move and was rarely rejected. How could I not be attracted to that kind of boldness? Friends warned me that I would run the risk of losing my virginal reputation, stating, "Birds of a feather . . . ," but I found Reese a refreshing change from those who pretended to be one thing in public but were another in private.

One afternoon I broke camp at fifth period so that my girl Reese could have sex with Howard, a fine redbone guy with curly hair and not much personality. I sat in his living room as his brother Ralph, ten years older, tried to get in my pants.

"It's just sex. What are you afraid of?" he insisted.

"Aren't you too old to be trying to sleep with sixteen-year-olds?" I shot back.

"I'm not thirty yet," he scoffed. "Come on you'll like it," he begged.

For the slightest moment I wondered if I could enjoy something so intimate with someone I despised. Two years earlier, I had spent a night listening to him spewing the same lines to a friend who, unlike me, had believed him. Even at sixteen, I thought he needed to stop using recycled game and come up with some fresh material. Either that or he needed to grow the fuck up and stay off the playground.

So I was relieved when a pissed-off Reese flew into the room, barely giving me time to collect my book bag. I raced after her, long chocolate legs flying down the dirt road.

She turned to me, furious, and spat out, "Man don't try to satisfy you, then fuck him. It ain't worth your time."

She stopped in midrant, turned, and faced me. "Shit, from now on I'm going first. Always get yours first."

And she took off again, with me hustling to keep up. Even if I got punished for cutting school, that tidbit of womanly advice was gold.

Between cutting classes, failing grades, and being unprepared, I got so many demerits that they booted me off the cheerleading squad. My mother, more absent even than before, didn't notice I had been kicked off the squad, or she would surely have gloated. I was raising myself and doing a horrible job, but despite everything else, somehow I managed to keep my virginity, settling instead for heavy petting sessions. I didn't let anyone love me or even get close enough to really know me. How could I?

Then I fell hard for a boy who functioned outside our circle; he was a nerd, and we were more mainstream. My friends told me not to waste my time, but I could be myself with him, and I never had to worry about him putting the moves on me. Instead we talked about our lives and our struggles. Neither of us was as well off as most of the popular kids. He was different than all the other boys I knew; he was raised by a single mother, and instead of running wild he took care of his younger brother and had real grown-up responsibilities. But I caved in to peer pressure, and I left him behind.

I also started hanging out with a black girl who only hung around the preppy white kids. Her father was a doctor, and she had moved from Maine and had never gone to school with black kids before. She was concerned with her weight and turned me on to uppers and acid. She told me all the different ways to keep from gaining extra pounds. Although I wasn't yet concerned about my weight, I did think to store the information just in case I needed it later.

In the late 1970s I, like many people, had never heard of eating disorders. It was obvious how unhappy my new friend was about her weight and how the notion of thinness consumed her thoughts. So looking back I can safely say that she either had an eating disorder or was on the road to one. She was in the drama club with me and eventually started dating a white boy until he caved from the pressure, as I had done with my nerd friend, and dumped her. At that point she became even more obsessed with her weight.

I then started dating a guy, Sheldon, who went to another school. Since I'd been raised in matriarchal environments, where women reined supreme, dating him proved difficult for me. According to him, if I were going to be his woman, I had to respect him as a man, and that meant letting him be the boss of me. He expected to know my every move and became angry when I denied him access or wasn't waiting at home for his call.

One night Sheldon, I, and another couple went to a football game. Sheldon had been drinking, which made him even more aggressive and controlling.

In the backseat he told me, "You need to start listening to me before I have to teach you your place."

My mouth always had a life of its own, and that night was no different. "Don't tell me what to do, Sheldon, you are not my father."

SLAP!

His large, heavy hand swung across my face, sending me reeling from the shock. I shrank back in fear. No man had ever dared to strike me, and it had been years since the last beating from my mother. I threw my hands up to cover my face, backing into a corner.

Sheldon sprang into apology mode, but I wasn't hearing him. "Don't touch me!" I could see my girlfriend's shocked face in the rearview mirror. "Let me out of this car," I screamed.

We were parked one building away from my house, and I hoped my mother had fallen asleep. Since it was way past my curfew, I didn't want to risk waking her as I slid out of the car.

"Girl, you OK?" my friend asked. "He hit you?"

But I couldn't answer because Sheldon stood blocking the entrance to my driveway.

"Please, baby, let me just talk to you. I'm sorry," he pleaded.

Even though I wanted to curse him out, reminding him that if he had kept his hands to himself he wouldn't have to be sorry, I played it cool, not wanting to set him off again. Clearly he was crazy, and I didn't want to risk his wrath by breaking up at that moment.

"Look, I'm tired and I just want to go home," I said.

"But I love you, Stephanie," he pleaded again.

"We're fine, Sheldon. Just let me go home," I insisted.

"You gonna break up with me?" he asked, and the threat was there.

"No, I'm just past my curfew so I got to go," I explained.

"Give me a hug then." He held out his arms, arms I wanted to flee. I relented and went into his arms, allowing him to feel forgiven. "I'll call you tomorrow," he said and smiled.

He grabbed my face, kissing me as I choked down the bile I wanted to spit at him. He stepped out of my path, and I raced to the safety of my front door. And as much as I usually hated coming home, at the moment it was the only place I wanted to be.

The next morning my phone rang off the hook with nosy people wanting to know about Sheldon beating me. So much for friends keeping their big mouths shut. I avoided his calls all weekend, grateful he and I didn't attend the same school.

At school on Monday word quickly spread about Sheldon putting his hands on me. The retold version had him slapping and choking me to within an inch of my life. After school I placed my things in my locker and headed up the stairs to drama club just as Sheldon came down the stairs, obviously searching for me. I gasped, my eyes darting around for an escape. He threw his hands in the air.

"I'm not going to touch you, I promise," he said.

"What do you want?" I backed away.

"Stephanie, can't we talk? I love you."

I shook my head. "I don't want your kind of love." I tried to dismiss him but he blocked my path.

"It will never happen again," he promised.

"I can't, Sheldon. I just can't," I told him.

"I'll never hit you again," he declared, his voice raising, threatening again.

"Stay away from me." I brushed past him as I hurried up the steps.

"That's it?" he asked.

"You hit me, Sheldon. You hit me . . . ," I wailed as I faded back from him. That's when I realized that getting hit was the bottom line for me.

That next summer before I turned seventeen, I discovered that being beaten nearly half to death by a man didn't cover Renee's bottom line at all. Her teenage lover, Robert, had been freed from jail, and just as she had promised Renee was there to welcome him home. Before long, she set up house, got pregnant, and married him. Over time Robert began a lucrative drug-dealing business, controlling his organization with threats and violence. They moved into Park Hill, a housing project on Staten Island, where they joined my aunt Bonita, aunt Rita, aunt Clarissa, and uncle John, each living in separate buildings. At first Renee fought off Robert's heavy blows, but then she became expert at hiding the bruises. Even when she was pregnant with her first child, Robert beat Renee, but that was never enough reason for her leave him. Always she found an excuse for him, always she loved him more than herself.

While Renee allowed a man to physically abuse her, I chose bulimia, as if consciously choosing to abuse myself. I knew I would never allow another person, particularly a man, to treat me badly again. It would be years before I understood that my sister and I had simply chosen two different halves of the same whole in order to fix something broken within us. The trouble was each of us had chosen a crutch that had the power to destroy us. And if that wasn't enough, Cecilia was slowly slipping into a dependency on drugs.

Tragedies

Two tragedies occurred while my mother and I were living in Norfolk. Both confirmed my belief that life was not only unfair but cruel.

The safe father figure I had managed to find was snatched away through no fault of his own, and the cousin I had recently connected with and formed a close bond with was also taken. I could not help but view these two events as confirmation that my faulty DNA guaranteed me a life of abandonment and that there was nothing I could do to change that. And although these were the first deaths I experienced in my life, I was becoming all too familiar with tragedy and loss.

One evening I returned home to find out that my uncle Sonny, my aunt Susie's common-law husband of ten years, had had a heart attack and died. Sonny had always been the one protective father figure for me. He had a big smile, a bigger heart, and an unbelievable, infectious laugh. We were the two Scorpios in the family and always stood on the same side, with my aunt Susie, Deborah, Felicia, and Daniel taking the opposite side during our fun roughhousing. He always took life easily, never stressing, and added a much-needed safe male presence to all our lives. I had never doubted Sonny's love or his kindness. He could always be counted on to give me and Felicia quarters to spend at the corner bodega on chips, cookies, and ice cream.

I had never experienced grief before, but again, I had never lost a man who actually loved me. Like an episode in a bad ghetto sitcom, I broke down and became the only family member trying to throw myself into the casket alongside Sonny. The loss devastated me so much that I wanted to go along to the next place with him. My grandmother and aunt grabbed hold of me and explained that we were in the wrong funeral room and would have to go next door to view Sonny's body.

At the real ceremony, embarrassed by my earlier episode, I avoided jumping into the casket. The loss affected everyone in my family deeply. It would be years before my aunt began to recover from his sudden death. She believed that if you were lucky enough to have one great love in life, you should count your blessings, and Sonny had been that for her.

The next tragedy came just as suddenly. Lisa, my cousin on my father's side, only six months older than me, to whom I had grown close, passed out on the basketball court during a game. Nicknamed Pepsi by her friends, Lisa slipped into a coma and within days died. She had contracted spinal meningitis.

On the plane ride to New York for her funeral, my mother explained that since the school year was ending she needed me to stay and take care of my aunt Gerda, Lisa's mother. I arrived to find my aunt, my father, and my grandmother, Irene, whom I had never met.

Upon first sight, I hated this woman—her turned-up nose and superior attitude, inspecting me as if I were cattle. I recalled that it was this woman who suggested my father join the army instead of taking responsibility for me when my mother became pregnant. It took twelve years for him to show up and attempt to get to know me. My father never came back to my mother, and even my aunt Gerda agreed it was his mother's influence that slanted his decision.

"Hello, Louise." Her cold, clipped tone greeted my mother and cemented her future with me. I loved my mother and could be fiercely protective of her. My sisters and I agreed; we could talk about our mother, but let anybody else—family or not— say one bad thing about her, and we would level them. My mother's middle name was Louise, and it was the name she reserved for people she liked or those who cared for her. Mary, her first name, was the one found on bills and work correspondence. The tone of this woman's voice made it unnatural for her to use my mother's more familiar moniker.

Having lost her favorite female granddaughter, my grandmother grabbed me in an embrace, smashing me to her sizable bosom, ready for me to step into Lisa's role. But I wasn't Lisa, and she had not loved me from birth.

"You look just like Conrad and Gerda," my grandmother purred, referring to my father and aunt.

Over that weekend she worked hard to thaw my resistance to her. "Stephanie, I will help you through college. How are your grades?" she pushed, wanting to catch up on my entire sixteen years in five minutes.

It did not take long to see that this matriarch expected control of her flock, and I had now been welcomed in, given carte blanche invitation to visit her in Florida or at her place in St. Thomas in the Virgin Islands. She let me know that money was no object, but already at my age I knew that even golden handcuffs were still handcuffs.

After the funeral I stayed in New York, and my mother returned to Norfolk and her comrades, and Cousin Dorie went back to school. I made sure Aunt Gerda ate and had everything she needed. I think it comforted her having another sixteen-year-old around who belonged to her. I loved being away from the empty refrigerator in Virginia; at my aunt's I did all the shopping and cooking with the money she gave me. It was the first time that I had freedom and money to make decisions in the grocery store and to eat whatever I craved day and night.

Losing Sonny and Lisa to death while losing my mother to her politics left me feeling lonelier and more abandoned than ever before. I fought to stay in New York, where I could live with Aunt Gerda and be close to Felicia and my sisters, but nothing I said could change my mother's mind. I belonged to my mother, and grief or no grief I had to return to her.

Once I landed back in Virginia, it soon became apparent that something had changed in me. School became one more thing that did not matter anymore. I was rebelling against my powerlessness to live the life I wanted where I would have been taken care of.

My grades and my attendance continued to slide. My mother didn't seem to care if I ate, so why would I expect her to care if I got good grades? I remember taking an IQ test in elementary school and the teacher informing my mother that I was genius level. My intellect was always something I took for granted, like the darkness of my skin. School had always been easy for me, something I never had to work at, and now that arrogance came at a price. I showed up at school unprepared or not at all.

One day the assistant principal, a serious black man, called me into his office.

"Stephanie, you are in jeopardy of flunking out of school and not graduating. We need to arrange a meeting with your mother," he said.

Immediately I envisioned the scene that could result. Even though my mother had neglected me, she would never stand for my skipping school. There in front of me sat my folder, filled to the brim with my misdeeds. I panicked, and my imagination and loose tongue slipped into overdrive.

"It's just that my life has been difficult lately." I sobbed real tears.

"I have to call your mother in for a talk," he explained.

"Please," I began, panic continuing to rise, "you don't understand."

"Then make me understand how someone with your intelligence has gone from having a decent academic record to flunking in two semesters. You hardly come to school, and when you do your attitude disrupts the entire class."

"I know . . . it's just that . . ." I struggled to find an excuse good enough to keep my mother in the dark. Tears flowed down my face, but his expression remained unchanged. "It's my mother—she beats me, and I'm afraid that if she comes to the school I don't know what she will do." I shuddered.

Thankfully, my mother had recently left her job as a school-bus driver, so he would not be running into her.

"She beats you?" he asked.

I struggled to find words powerful enough to save me. "She sleeps with men for money," I spat out, "and she drinks . . . a lot . . . and when she gets angry . . ." I burst into uncontrollable sobs, terrified my lie wouldn't work and even more afraid that it would be repeated to my mother.

But the assistant principal could not believe anyone would lie to such an extreme; he bought my act.

"I'm scared of her," I whimpered, my body shaking in fear. I glanced up at him, his face a mask of concern, and I knew I was safe.

"You're going to have to have a study hall," he offered, "and no more cutting class."

"Thank you," I squeaked out, tears falling, relieved that my mother wouldn't find out. Lucky for me this was back before schools had rules to call social workers at the first sign that a kid was in trouble at home.

That weekend, my mother and Bob were away on some protest march, and they left my cousin Greg to watch me. On Friday Reese and I took hits of acid—my first—licking the cartoon characters until we were tripping. We had tickets to see Angie B and Grandmaster Flash and the Furious Five. Reese and I, all of seventeen, firm and juicy, stopped by the Norfolk State campus apartment where Greg hung with his boys, ready for a party. The boys couldn't believe their luck, but Greg, ever in the role of protective big brother, was having none of that and admonished us for being scantily clad and feeling ourselves.

"Can I spend the night at her house? My mother lets me," I pleaded.

Greg, always a softy, gave in. "Be home by noon tomorrow and don't make me come looking for you," he demanded.

Reese and I exchanged winks as we switched out the door high on acid.

At the Norfolk Scope Arena we quickly made our way through the crowds. Reese—long legs, skirt hiked up to her butt cheeks—rarely heard the word no. She knew how to use her body to get what she wanted, and she wanted to go back-stage. The leering security guard complied, hustling us back-stage as fresh meat for the hungry pack of rappers.

Reese was in her element, as the rappers vied for her atten-tion. She chose a tall, lanky, chocolaty one. I, less experienced but emboldened by the drugs coursing through my veins, went for the cute one. He went straight to the point without any pre-tense of affection or romance, just straight-up desire.

"Want to spend the night with me?" He threw it out there.

"I'm a virgin," I said.

He studied my half-naked woman-child body, then threw his head back and laughed in disbelief. "Is that a yes?"

His dimples pushed me over that edge. We drank, got high, and danced around backstage, having a party.

Angie B, the baddest female rapper of her day, pulled me aside. "Child, you ain't got no business being here. Where your momma?" She took her big-sister thing seriously.

"I can hang," I stuttered, knowing she was absolutely right, but I had never had sex of my own free will, and this guy wasn't making promises he wasn't going to keep, and I found that liberating. Already, the thought of being in love, of being out of control, left me cold. I wanted no part of flowery love poems and false promises of forever. I knew the deal.

"These boys sleep with different women every night," Angie warned me. "They won't remember your name a week from now," she promised.

At that moment my mother's face flashed in my mind, and I knew what I wanted to do.

Shortly after my induction into womanhood, I grew even more frustrated with life in Virginia. I did not want to need my mother anymore. I believed that having sex proved that I wasn't a little girl anymore, and I was ready to make my own decisions and to stand on my own two feet—with help, of course.

So one afternoon I decided that I just could no longer take Virginia. My grades were floundering, I was sad all the time, and I just needed my extended family. While my mother was away on another protest march, I slipped my belongings into a bag, hopped a Greyhound bus, and headed back to New York. I knew I was out of control and couldn't rein myself in, but I knew that my family could.

I had expected my mother to be furious but also to feel abandoned. In her view, we had a close mother-daughter relationship, which meant I should have come to her before I did anything foolish. But in my view, she did all the talking, and I was simply her audience. Sure enough, I got the call, and she was pissed and hurt, but she didn't try to change my mind. Instead, she simply voiced her disappointment. Both my sisters had departed by my age, and there had been little she could do to keep them at home. I gave no indication that I would ever return.

Back in Brooklyn, I lived with my aunt in Park Slope, which we referred to simply as "the Slope." My aunt Susie was strict, and she had rules, which I was not used to. I had been free to run wild the last two years in Virginia.

Finally, my cousin Felicia and I were in the same school, but that didn't bond us the way I had expected. We were seventeen, and we each wanted to assert our independence in the world and from each other. We didn't like each other's friends, and although it was probably because we were each so used to being the center of the other's universe, neither welcomed the competition.

My new best friend was Liz Sanchez, who watched me turn up my nose at this inner-city school full of lack and dirt and called me a snob. As much as I protested my life in Virginia, once back in New York I realized that I had gotten used to a better quality of living, which included a clean, well-equipped public school.

"Who do you think you are, Miss Thing?" Liz shot at me.

Her open face and big smile caused all my defenses to crumble, and I had to laugh at myself. Liz's parents, Angel and Carmen, became my second family. Over *café con leche* and *arroz con pollo* I fell in love with the Sanchez family, and they welcomed me like their own flesh and blood. They were loud, boisterous, and argumentative, but they stuck together, and nothing, not even Angel Sr.'s occasionally fleeing to Puerto Rico, could separate them for long. Whenever I entered their apartment, where Liz's younger brothers Angel Jr. and Luis were always playing, Carmen would insist on feeding me.

"Stephanie, you and Liz are too skinny, you must eat," she'd insist, shoving a giant plate of food in my direction, and I was home.

And when Angel Sr. would get mad at the loud black kids in the neighborhood who disrespected him by leaning on his car, he'd rage, "I hate niggers," but he would always follow with, "But not you, Stephanie."

I couldn't get offended because I knew he had come from a different world, and the "n" word didn't hold as much weight for him as it did for me. Besides, they were my family, and they looked out for me, fed me, and wanted me to succeed in life.

After a while, feeling stifled by my aunt Susie's rules, I moved in with my aunt Rita, who lived in Flatbush in Brooklyn with her husband Bubba and her kids Nikky, Terrance, and Yolanda. I got a job at the Red Apple supermarket in Manhattan on Ninety-Ninth and Broadway so that I could afford to feed myself, which took precedence over everything else. Being able to feed myself was a sign of true independence for me. I could buy whatever I wanted: fast food, Chinese, pizza, knishes, pretzels, hero sandwiches. On the days I worked late I took care of my own food, even though my aunt always offered to leave a plate on the stove for me.

The luxury of a paycheck allowed me to pack on a few extra pounds, and I was not feeling that at all. I started to take diet pills and tried unsuccessfully to lead a Slim-Fast life, but I had no discipline when it came to diets. I couldn't stop eating junk food and all the treats that had been out of my reach for so long in Virginia. Fast food, which had always been too expensive, became my staple. This lasted until I got fired for stealing, one of the rare times I was wrongly accused. The only upside to unemployment was that I had to cut back on the junk food I could no longer afford. My weight had always fluctuated within the same ten pounds, always within a normal range. I stayed somewhere between one hundred and fifteen pounds and one hundred and twenty-five pounds.

But before long, I again packed my bags, this time moving in with my grandmother in her two-room apartment in the Fort Greene projects, further traumatizing my mother, who dropped an invitation to move back to Virginia into every conversation. To my mother, project doors swung one way—inward—but she should have had more faith in me. Coming back to New York from the middle-class world of Virginia, I no longer saw poverty as an option. In Virginia my friends were into college degrees and fashion labels; Aigner and Izod were standards I hadn't quite reached, but I knew that one day I would. My world had already expanded beyond the zone of the projects and the people in them. As far as I was concerned this stop was temporary.

Less than a week after moving in with my grandmother, I met my first real boyfriend, Dexter, when he was called on to repair the elevator in my grandmother's building. Tall, slim, and milk chocolate, he was twenty. Dexter's mother was an executive at the Housing Authority, and after one conversation with him I knew he was from a separate world. Dexter worked at night and went to college in the daytime. He had put himself on the path to law school, and I loved what appeared to be his ambition.

Dexter and I hung in the Village, taking in jazz clubs and eating ethnic foods. Dexter introduced me to Steely Dan, Michael Franks, and the Police. I did cut school a few times to travel to St. Albans in Queens where Dexter lived with his parents in a beautiful Tudor house.

I liked Dexter a lot, but once again a relationship with a man raised my doubts as to my ability to form any emotional connection. It never turned into love for me. He was skinny as a rail, and when he worked he stopped by my grandmother's on his dinner break. He'd always let it slip that he was hungry. And even though I could relate to this his hunger, I didn't understand it, because there was no crisis of finances. Dexter never worried about money; he always had it. He lived at home with two middle-class, working parents. He made more at his job than my mother had ever made at hers, and he kept a low overhead, his being the only mouth he had to feed. Dexter just liked the idea of someone taking care of him, and he loved the idea that it would be me. To him, a woman's love meant nurturing and caretaking, but I felt manipulated. It was never straightforward; he would say things like "Can you hear how empty my stomach is?"

So I began to take responsibility for his hunger, making sure I had a meal prepared when he stopped by. I had two dishes in my repertoire, so I mainly fixed breakfast. But it wasn't long before I began to resent being manipulated by Dexter, especially since he rarely kept any of the promises he made.

I rejoined the Henry Street Settlement, taking acting classes. I loved being among the artists and performers who considered Henry Street their second home. I also started to notice Dexter's preference for being high to attending school. Nothing turned me off quicker than lack of ambition, and Dexter's cardboard house of excuses why he couldn't finish things he'd started made it easy to dismiss him from my life. I refused to get trapped in the cycle of teen pregnancy and poverty that I came from. He was going nowhere on his own.

Part Two

During

On My Own

One year after graduating from high school I got a job working for Time-Life and took an apartment squarely on the other side of the tracks. I lived alone in a renovated one-bedroom on Atlantic Avenue near Flatbush. I had brick walls, a loft bed, a working fireplace, and a fourth-floor-walkup view of the Brooklyn Academy and the clock tower at the former Williamsburg Savings Bank.

I went through lots of romantic trials and tribulations, but I never fell for anyone. I loved my new life. It was during this time that I met a friend who would prove invaluable in my life—Elizabeth Smith, known as Beebe. She worked for Woody King Jr., and her husband, Fred, worked for the *MacNeil/Lehrer Report* and adored his wife, who never stopped moving. Beebe took me under her wing, teaching me etiquette and polishing my rough edges. She was also always willing to feed me and to introduce me to fancy restaurants. When she offered to teach me to cook, and I scoffed, feeling way too feminist for that, she explained, "You got to eat. Besides, it's one more thing to put in your repertoire." Beebe was a jill of all trades, and she catered large functions on the side. She hired me as a potato peeler and insisted I work my way up the cooking chain. It's because of her that I love cooking today.

Beebe hailed from Tulsa, Oklahoma, and had been Miss Black Oklahoma; she prided herself on good manners and chastised me for showing up empty handed at dinner parties. She also thought she was still in Oklahoma and spoke to strangers in the crowded Manhattan streets. Fred's family had a home in Sag Harbor in the Hamptons, which Beebe felt free to loan out to me at will. I often went to the Hamptons for the weekend, partying among people who summered and vacationed regularly. These were black people different than the ones I grew up with—they took regular trips to Europe, considering themselves Francophiles. But for me Sag Harbor was an escape from the city where I could write on the weekends and walk near the ocean without the noise of the city.

It was at this time that Beebe and I both received roles in Gertrude Jeanette's play *Light in the Cellar* at a theater in Harlem. Also appearing in the play was a guy named Gary, the son of a famous acting duo. The attraction between Gary and me was instantaneous and mutual. He had just starred in his first film, and we were all excited to have him in this production with us. Very laid-back and easygoing, he was not at all the spoiled crown prince we expected because of his famous parents.

Before long, our easy flirtation resulted in Gary inviting me to see him perform his blues music at a magic club in the Village. After a few dates it appeared Gary and I were headed somewhere. That is, until Beebe dropped out of the play and had to be replaced at a moment's notice.

I suggested an actress I knew from Henry Street. Teresa had a crush on my friend Clean and seemed harmless and fun. Because of the large cast, Gertrude rehearsed us on alternate days, with the exception of Gary and Jeffrey, who were the leads.

One night Gary, who had made plans to drop by after his performance at an East Village club, called to inform me he would be late because Teresa had surprised him by showing up at the club.

Now I can smell a rat a mile away, and I knew Teresa's appearance meant she wanted him. Not one to back down from a confrontation, I got cute, jumped on the train, and hustled to the club myself.

As much as I hated to admit it, I had begun to fall for Gary. All the time we had spent alone, talking and sharing our feelings, had made me vulnerable, more than I had ever allowed myself to be before. To say Gary was not happy to see me was putting it mildly.

"You don't own me, Stephanie," he hissed.

I gave him a look that let him know I actually didn't care to own him. But like a bitch in heat, I had marked my territory, and Teresa knew I was dating Gary and should have acted accordingly. Teresa lived on the Lower East Side, but that night Gary traveled out of his way, across the bridge, and dropped me off first to prove some kind of point. I fought back tears as Teresa smugly slid into my front seat, next to Gary, as he pulled away from the curb.

How could I have let my guard down and allowed myself to like any man that much? The next week Teresa purred to me at rehearsal, "I like Gary, and if he asks me I am going to continue dating him. I think we'd make a good couple."

My Scorpion tongue, never at a loss for a comeback, struck. "Teresa, if you want Gary, you can have him. Men are like buses, and there is always another one coming around the corner," I said sweetly before flouncing off.

At the next rehearsal, Gary was waiting for me. He grabbed me by the arm, pulling me into the hallway, breathing fire. "How dare you! Who do you think you are, giving me away? You don't own me."

"Look, I just told Teresa that if she wants you she can have you," I retorted. I stared at him, annoyance showing on my face.

He stormed back into the rehearsal space. I had won whatever fight we were having, and I knew it.

Less than a week later, Gary showed up on my doorstep confessing he had begun to fall in love with me and asking for a second chance. Instead of maintaining the icy exterior I had learned to put up when confronted with a vulnerable situation, I let down my defenses. I admitted to Gary that I had begun to fall in love with him, too. Gary would be the first man I ever loved, and he proved harder to get over than any before or since. He was the first man to take responsibility for the care and feeding of me. He and I became a "we," functioning in our own world, separate from everyone else. We rarely hung out with others, preferring to stay cloistered in our own twosome, and I was in heaven.

We spent alternate weekends at his parents', where he lived in a separate apartment on the top floor of their home. While his dad liked anybody and everybody, Gary's mother was also a Scorpio and never warmed to the idea of her thirty-six-year-old son dating a free-spirited twenty-one-year-old. By that young age my independence had solidified in a way that Gary's never had. The only time he had ever lived apart from his parents was when he had moved out of state, and that didn't last long. But a year after meeting me, he was living in the apartment vacated by my mother. A year after I graduated high school my mother had moved to Newark, a couple of years later she'd relocated to the Cloisters neighborhood in Manhattan, and now she was off to a new life in Boston. I had pushed Gary toward independence, insisting he take over my mother's lease. I liked his family, but I wanted him to stand on his own two feet . . . with me.

I was working at Time-Life in the accounts payable department, something I managed to do really badly. While I loved the steady paycheck, it didn't work with my new artist's lifestyle. As much as I craved the stability, I wanted to create, to write and even to act if it afforded me the freedom to write. Sunday to Thursday nights I hung out, dancing at the Limelight, Danceteria, Area, the Paradise Garage, or the Palladium, and then heading off to after-hours underground clubs until four in the morning. I'd stumble into my job, coffee in hand, pushing papers, reading numbers, while my boss wondered how I had gotten the job in the first place. Finally, I quit because I knew it wouldn't be long before I got that pink slip anyway. I went off to work at a talent management company that represented kids. The company was run by an older woman who worked out of her spacious apartment on Riverside Drive. We sent caffeinated stage mothers and their precious offspring into the lion's den of show business every day, and they couldn't get enough of the auditions. Working at this job allowed me to pursue my real passion, playwriting. I loved writing, but I didn't think I was educated enough to do it for a living. I didn't believe it could be anything more than a hobby. I also liked the artist's lifestyle—the money wasn't consistent, but the freedom to maneuver satisfied me.

I had grown up watching the adults in my life work jobs they hated for a modest paycheck and no job security. I decided early that since I only had the guarantee of this life, I owed it to myself to do what I really enjoyed. I couldn't be my family, struggling an entire lifetime to get to the middle.

Around this time my mother fell madly, passionately in love with a blond nurse named Jane, a relationship ultimately more damaging than any she'd had with a man. Suddenly my mother hung out a lesbian multicolored banner, causing my sisters to lose it.

My sisters, for all their modern women crap, were as old-fashioned as 1950s housewives. Cecilia, at twenty-three, hadn't yet gotten her first job, instead choosing to depend on the kind-

ness of boyfriends taken with her beauty and charm (read: sex).
She bartered her looks for love, comfort, and eventually the
necessary escapism of drugs. Renee, still married to Robert,
could never admit to him that her mother slept with women,
and kept it a secret. I couldn't believe such closed-minded girls
were my mother's daughters. To tease them, I'd rattle off sexual
proclivities of lesbians that sent them over the edge while I
laughed hysterically at their shock.

I accepted my mother's lesbianism, considering it one more
way she separated herself from the pack. And after all it seemed
a natural transition from a white man.

"She went from a white man to a white woman!" my sisters
raged. Neither would ever cross the color barrier, seeing nothing attractive that wasn't black.

My mother never actually came out to us. Instead she
dropped Jane's name into every conversation, like a water bal-
loon, a pretty little toy capable of exploding in the heat.

"Jane came over . . ." "Jane and I . . ." "Me and Jane . . ."
and on and on. It didn't take a psychology degree to figure out
that my mother's insertion of Jane in every conversation was
her attempt to get us to warm to this relationship, but that
never actually happened. I wondered if her relationship with
Jane would have fared better if she had introduced Jane in a
less passive-aggressive manner. Two years later, still waving
the multicolored lesbian banner, my mother, sans Jane, moved
to New Jersey. Their relationship had ended with restraining
orders and false accusations on both parts. That alone would
have cured me of lesbianism, but once my mother was committed to something she hung in there whether it made sense
or not. In fact, the less sense it made, the deeper my mother
devoted herself to it. It was so like my mother to take the path
of most resistance. Later I asked my mother if she had been
lesbian pre-Jane, to which she replied, "No, I met a woman and
fell in love. I never really thought about being gay before, but
being with her made sense." After the relationship imploded
I expected my mother to revert back to heterosexuality like

one of those four-year lesbians attending liberal arts colleges in the Northeast, but that didn't happen. My mother became antimale, vocal in discouraging her daughters against men and marriage. The track records of women in my family having successful relationships with men did not bode well for any of us. The Covington women and love seemed at odds, but it didn't stop any of us from being hopeful and diving in time and time again. That's the thing about some men—once you get a taste you can spend your entire life chasing after them, even if there is nothing there.

Losing It

The words *I love you* always rang hollow for me, even though hearing them became my obsession. They were one part heaven, two parts hell. Cornered, staring up into the face of some hopelessly romantic man, I always muttered them back. On those countless times I said *I love you*, I had no connection to the words. I couldn't conjure up the feelings. I'd listen to my sisters and friends skipping happily over the words, enthused to be transported by them to some magical place. I wondered why my real reaction, the one I kept to myself, was so different. When a boy professed his love, painting a picket fence around our future, I began to slowly back away, to find fault with him, to wish him gone. *Poof!* I'd behave like a passenger with a fear of flying trapped inside a 747. Panicking, I'd watch the exits, listening carefully to the flight attendant as she rattled off the emergency evacuation procedure, unable to breathe properly until the plane landed and I was back on the ground. I could never get comfortable in my seat or in myself. I could never relax, never allow a man to love me.

Why did something as sweet as a man confessing his love send me into a claustrophobic panic? It didn't matter who the man was; those words made me feel nothing but trapped. To my ears, they sounded like a death sentence. The only man I ever wanted to love me, my father, didn't, and the parade of young men who came after him tried but couldn't fill the phantom space he held in my life. I unknowingly punished men for not being able to replace what I really needed, a father. This need had created an insatiable hunger for love and validation, but after I achieved the Holy Grail—a man's love—I wasn't comfortable until I destroyed it. Because I believed I was unlovable at my core, I couldn't trust that a man would love me. I'd push and push and push until one of us fled in another direction, or I grew to despise anyone who chose me. Like Groucho Marx, I didn't want to be a member of any club that would have me. Unfortunately for those men who tried to love me, it would be years before therapy awakened me to the depth of my issues with relationships, before I recognized how my self-loathing kept me from being intimate. And more years before I learned to trust and accept that I could be loved.

During that period of my life, the only man who ever came close was Gary. But he didn't come just as an individual; he brought along a large extended family with protective arms strong enough to shelter me from painful childhood memories. For a time, the security of their consistency wiped away years of my wanting to belong to normal. Their sense of family felt like a gigantic swell, carrying me up in a wave of contentment, of sisters and lifelong friendships and parents whose places at the head of the table allowed the rest of the family to feel safe. Unlike the fairy-tale family I created in my head at night to lull myself to sleep, Gary's parents were living, breathing people who loved their children without question. Losing Gary meant losing an extended family and my newfound sense of normalcy. To whom could I retreat? Where could I go to feel safe without the glare of weirdness? Who would love me?

Gary and I began to unravel mainly because of my need for more. My need for him to prove his love was insatiable. No amount of assurance could satisfy my hunger for security. We spent every free waking moment together, merging easily, so I felt marriage was the next logical step. Even though I knew he loved me, I wanted more, so I kept pushing.

And he broke up with me. I had never been in love before and was completely unprepared for the lack of control I felt. In the words of my grandmother, I had put all my eggs in one basket, and when they began to crack so did I.

Nothing had prepared me for the resurgence of pain and the sense of abandonment from my childhood that hit me when Gary left. All those years I had stood back, baffled by and scoffing at the feelings of love my sisters, cousins, and friends felt for the men in their lives. In the past, even when I tried to care, I felt nothing when a relationship was over or a man told me he didn't love me. I seemed incapable of caring past the expiration date on the milk carton, and often I had moved on before then. Sure, sometimes my ego got involved, because I always wanted to be the one who left first. My sentiments were like those *Our Gang* television shows that played on Saturday mornings, in which the sour-faced loser always professed, "Love is for suckers." Nothing could convince me to fall deeply enough to expose myself to hurt. And here, suddenly, because of a man, like the lovelorn women in my life whom I had scoffed at, I was an emotional mess, a stranger to myself.

An avalanche of pain and loss toppled me, rendering me devastated in a dark and unfamiliar place. Many of the women on my mother's side of the family had at one time or another attempted suicide, and now I, too, became suicidal.

I turned on the oven in my apartment, and I called Gary to tell him I was going to kill myself, begging him one last time to rush to my rescue. I wanted him to realize that he loved me too much to leave.

And before I knew it, the fire department appeared at my door and carted me off to Bellevue.

"Do you like Sylvia Plath novels?"

A pubescent doctor had ordered a psych evaluation, and the questions being asked were so obvious. I wasn't an idiot; I knew that answering yes to inquiries such as this would ensure a lockdown with padded walls and scary roommates. I gave practiced, sane-girl answers to the psychologist's questions, contrary to the thoughts swirling inside my head, the details of which would have exceeded the requirements of the standard forty-eight-hour evaluation. At the time, it didn't even occur to me that my own mother had passed through these same doors years earlier when she had been committed for a postbreakup breakdown.

"You really should see a therapist. Talk to someone about your feelings so they don't stay pent up and you explode," the psychologist suggested.

Where I come from, only the clinically diagnosed crazies went to a therapist. Besides, who could afford it? Normal black women were born equipped to deal with the stress of their lives, and I decided I would be no different. I would be strong, just as I was expected to be.

I thanked the doctor for taking the time to evaluate me and being helpful. I played him like a musical instrument, hitting every note, and I was granted freedom.

When I emerged from the heavily guarded psych section into the waiting room and toward the exit looming ahead, it was not Gary I found, but my father. He looked exhausted, as if he too had been up all night answering questions. He embraced me awkwardly; the extent of our touching to that point had been handshakes.

I couldn't believe that the man who had rarely shown up for me in twenty-one years had arrived at my most vulnerable moment. But even the shock of his presence and his offer of comfort did not break through my tough exterior. In so many ways he was still a stranger. To say I had the capacity to shift and let my father in would be yet another lie; I steeled myself against his presence.

"You all right?" he asked.

Of course, my standing in the waiting room of Bellevue Hospital, narrowly escaping admittance, kind of answered that question, but, understanding his discomfort, I did the only thing I could and lied. "I'm fine. I was just upset."

"We're going to go to my place and get some rest," my father informed me.

On the subway ride to the Bronx I fell asleep on my father, something I'd wanted my whole childhood. Since his recent divorce from his second wife, my father had become more available. His barely furnished apartment screamed "temporary" and included only a couch and a bedroom set.

Years later my father would remarry his ex-wife Brenda and sever all ties to his family forever: his parents, his only sibling my aunt Gerda, my brother Jasen, and me. But that night we stayed up talking, me leaning into my father, his body stiffened against my weight, not allowing me to get comfortable. Gently, at first, he tried to separate himself from me as I sobbed, soaking his shirt, relieved at twenty-one to be the daughter in her daddy's arms.

"Uh . . . ," he began, his increasing discomfort obvious until he clumsily separated himself from me as if he'd gotten static shock. "It's just that you don't seem like a daughter to me, Stephanie. You seem like a woman." His discomfort and words implied that he felt a frightening sexual chemistry between us.

And just like a record scratching to a stop, my father's words ended my fantasy of being loved by him. He had become one more man whose words and deeds blurred the boundaries of appropriate behavior. I decided then and there that I no longer needed a father. Early the next morning as my father slept, I snuck away, taking the train back to Brooklyn.

The next day I purchased a backpack, filled it to overflowing, and left my apartment. I took the F train to the Forty-Second Street Port Authority. At the ticket window I checked the destinations, choosing the place farthest away from New York and Gary.

"Portland, Oregon," I told the clerk. "Can I get off the bus anywhere I want?"

"You can use this ticket for the next sixty days. So as long as you arrive at your destination in sixty days, you're fine," he informed me.

On the bus I met other backpackers, mostly teenage foreigners trekking across America. I learned about youth hostels and surviving on a budget, but mostly I felt alone as I meandered from city to city—Philadelphia, Chicago, Denver, Las Vegas. I ignored my life, my family, and my friends back in New York. In my pained, self-involved state I didn't call anyone, convinced that no one cared.

Finally, about six days later I phoned Clean, my play brother whom I'd known since childhood. He could always be counted on to bail me out of trouble. He and his wife were as close as family. Gary and I had just taken part in Clean's wedding, so it was safe to assume a conversation between he and Gary had taken place, the story ending with me being carted off to the psych ward.

"Stephanie." I could hear the relief in his voice. It hadn't occurred to me that someone might have lain awake, afraid I had jumped off the Brooklyn Bridge days ago. "Where are you?"

"I'm in Las Vegas on my way to Portland. Next stop is Los Angeles, so I'll probably bum around there for a day or two," I confessed.

"Take this number, it's my friend Tony. He lives in L.A. Call him and tell him you're my little sister and he has to take care of you," he insisted. "Phone him as soon as we hang up and let him know you're coming," he ordered.

I called Tony, but he wasn't around, so his roommate Donald gave me the address and directions. Taking a cue from my mother, I believed that a geographical shift would fix all of my problems, and sunny California appeared to be a perfect solution.

Hollywood, California

Travel weary and suddenly hopeful, I arrived in Hollywood on a Tuesday, a thin film of smog layering the once-blue sky. I mistakenly got off the bus in downtown Los Angeles, a dirty, semideserted neighborhood where bad cop chases were simulated for television shows, an area that could resemble any other city. I took the Sunset bus to Hollywood, whose seediness resembled a hooker stroll in any eighties cop drama. I walked the six blocks to Tony's place on Holly Drive, a standard 1970s motel-style apartment, the kind found from one end of lower-income Los Angeles to the other.

At the door Fed, a white, overweight pothead, greeted me as if it were perfectly normal for a twenty-one-year-old black woman who hadn't bathed in a week to expect to crash on his couch. Donald, a hot, blond actor/waiter, arrived home soon, speaking with a Southern twang and making sure I had everything I needed. Much later, Tony, a tall, good-looking biracial bohemian, found me half asleep on the couch.

"You're Clean's little sister? Cool. How is he?" he asked. "Hungry?"

Three young, single guys, and not one seemed at all fazed by my sudden appearance. If this were New York City—at least my New York—there wouldn't be an open-door policy unless you were a blood relative, and even then it might not work out in your favor. But here, by the morning I had my own set of keys and directions to all sites Hollywood.

Two weeks later I returned to New York to pack my things, and, with the blessings of the guys, within a month I had moved to California. New York held too many reminders of the life I would never have with Gary. I either had no self-esteem or a big enough dose to rule the world as I bid New York good-bye. With twenty dollars in my pocket and a blissful ignorance I began my new life in Los Angeles. I got a list of talent agencies, hoping to land a job as a talent-management assistant. Each day I trekked five to ten miles searching for work, and before long I had whittled myself down to a magical size 2. For the first time in my life I didn't care if I ate or not; in fact, I had no desire for food at all (read: depression). I felt phenomenal.

My first California dating experience wound up being typical L.A. Strolling down Sunset Boulevard, I noticed a bright red small-penis car, a Ferrari, pull up alongside me. Ralph flirted shamelessly, his self-deprecating humor more of a turn-on than the ridiculous midlife-crisis mobile he drove. He talked me into a dinner date, which wasn't difficult, because after two weeks pounding the pavement and living on bagels the idea of a white tablecloth, a smiling waiter in a penguin suit, and meat and vegetables seemed heavenly.

He picked me up in the loud red car, my three male roommates encouraging me to have a great time in the hope that the rides would extend in their direction. Being a New York City public-transport girl, I saw cars as useful only for getting from one venue to the next without having to deal with overcrowded trains and their smells. But in L.A. cars were a confirmation or rejection of your social status. Over dinner Ralph told me about the Century City law firm he co-owned, and the law he practiced, one step above ambulance chaser. Ralph had the kind of blond boyish looks that made it impossible to pinpoint the decade of his birth. I figured forty to fifty as a realistic age range for him. After a week of dating he introduced me to his house, a beautiful Spanish hacienda with massive doors that he had personally imported from Morocco, hand-painted tile flooring, a pool, a sauna, and a view of Hollywood.

As he droned on about the cost and quality of his material objects, including the Maserati in the garage, his tone darkened. "Stephanie, I've worked hard for all my things. Why, today I bought myself a sixteen-hundred-dollar sweater," he boasted, showing me a garment a little too Cosby for my taste.

"Oh, that's nice," I murmured, taking in the sweeping city views.

"You don't seem to understand how wonderful it is to be able to buy anything you want." He dangled the bait.

"As long as you're happy, Ralph." My words fell like leaden weights.

"You wouldn't want to go shopping wherever you wanted, eat wherever you liked, and never have to worry about money? You telling me that you wouldn't prefer to live here?" His frustration with me became more evident because I didn't jump at his offer.

"No, I'm OK where I am." I fought the feeling of being offended. It reminded me of the time in grade school when another student made fun of my poverty by laughing at my single pair of high-quality but worn-down shoes. But now, instead of going all ghetto and cursing out the person trying to make me feel ashamed or struggling or needy, I stayed calm and listened.

"You like living in that dump?" he went on. Nothing in him could understand my refusal to leap at the lifestyle upgrade he held out for me.

"Yeah, I like it. I'm twenty-two and I don't need my life to be any certain way, I just need to be happy." I chose my words carefully, as if talking to a child on the brink of a tantrum, which he was quickly nearing.

"That's ridiculous," he scoffed.

"No, it's not. What would be ridiculous is letting some man take care of me because I don't want to do it myself," I lashed out.

"So you'd rather live in a dump with no car, looking for some minimum-wage job?" he barked.

He didn't comprehend that I had just begun a new life in a new city and I loved every moment of it. For God's sake, I had moved to California, and the last thing I wanted was a man looking to control me. Unlike a lot of women flocking to the City of Angels I wanted to make my own dreams come true. Besides, I knew that there was no such thing as an easy ride; I knew his offer, just like my grandmother's invitations, was a set of handcuffs disguised as an expensive bracelet.

A week later, while dining at Lawry's steakhouse on La Cienega's restaurant row, Ralph blew his top when I ordered my steak well done.

"Nobody orders a steak well done."

"Well I do," I answered, probably a little too sassy for his taste. I had already grown sick of Ralph trying to teach me the proper ways to eat, speak, and behave, as if I were a monkey he was trying to train. The only reason I continued these dinner dates was to bring back doggie bags full of goodies to my hungry roommates, who allowed me to live rent free. Ralph stiffened as I issued a glare meant to annoy him even more. No way was I trading youth for money, even if I starved to death. So that ended my first dating experience in L.A.

After a month of searching for work, I got a job a few blocks from my temporary housing in Hollywood, working for a bogus talent agency, one of those businesses that people warn you about in Hollywood. This company made its money hustling half-cute kids with desperate parents who believed their offspring were gifted. These parents plunked down good money that could have been better allocated to real-life necessities to enroll in the agency's star-making program (read: scam). They offered classes, head shots that cost a small fortune, and introductions to major talent agencies in Hollywood.

The owner's son had been in a few blockbusters and was still a viable commodity, his career owing nothing to his father, who nevertheless milked the association, leading these naive parents to believe their kids could become as famous as his son. Years later, as the movie star son's career tanked due to drugs and out-of-control behavior, I wondered if the father was still using his son as a shining example of his influence. The problem with the program, which I learned shortly after joining the company, was that all the cute kids the owner promised to help never had their head shots leave the file cabinets. Lots of them were talented and easily could have become successful if the shot he offered had been legitimate. After discovering that my real job consisted of fielding phone calls from angry parents raging about how they had been duped, I knew I had to exit. I quit, but not before an angry father entered the offices and attacked the owner, whose slick, fancy talk couldn't compete with the heavy fist of a disgruntled parent.

My mother, although relieved that I had moved to California, worried about me being so far away from family and insisted that I call my aunt Gerda, who had moved to Pasadena three years earlier to marry her boyfriend. That relationship had gotten my aunt to California but fizzled shortly after her arrival. Choking back my pride, I phoned my aunt, my only relative living in California, wondering if she'd hang up, since our last conversation years earlier, after I'd turned eighteen, had not gone well. I'd thought I was grown up and said as much to my aunt when she disapproved of my dating choice. Even though she was right, I couldn't bring myself to admit that I wasn't old enough to make smart decisions. My pride had cost me years of a having a better connection with her.

The relief in her voice was evident. It took a moment to remember that when last we spoke I had been tripping down the path of welfare, baby daddies, and limitations, and here I had arrived sane and sound in Los Angeles, supposedly freed of my youthful, impulsive, self-destructive behavior. When I explained that I lived with three men in a questionable section of Hollywood, Aunt Gerda suggested rather firmly that she pick me up the next night for dinner.

One look at the peeling powder-blue building with Donald's broken-down Beemer parked in the driveway and my couch-as-bedroom situation sent my aunt into rescue mode.

"I think you should come live with me," she offered. I had just gotten a job at the Gage Group talent agency in Beverly Hills, and the trek from Pasadena was lengthy, but at the same time a clean place to live with privacy and food could not be ignored. Sensing my hesitancy, my aunt let me know that her offer was not optional.

"No niece of mine is living like this. You can stay with me until you get on your feet," she said, and that settled that. I relocated to her two-bedroom townhouse in Pasadena.

Martin Gage was a larger-than-life character straight out of some old Hollywood movie, with shocking white hair, a bit of a whine to his voice, and a gift for getting actors and executives alike to bend to his will.

"Bubba, can you get me such and such on the phone?" he'd plead. "Dahling, its Marty, how're the kids?" and off he'd be, reminding some studio head that he or she had gotten his or her start answering the phones on Martin's front desk before requesting a favor the executive obligingly gave. In Hollywood there was an unspoken rule that someone would do you a favor, but eventually you would be called on to repay that favor, so it was best to repay it with a smile. People loved Martin because he was fair and generous and had a long history in show business, but it was kind of like the uncle who brought you great presents but with the unspoken expectation that you'd show up for dinner once a month to listen to his war stories.

Within a month I became part of the Gage Group family, working with such rising stars as Tim Robbins and Woody Harrelson. When Geraldine Page, one of our clients, received her Oscar, notoriously frugal Martin gave bonuses to the entire office, including me, who'd only been there a month.

My slight dyslexia with numbers forever had me on the agents' shit list. "Calpurnia, can you get a number correct?" an agent would complain, using my new nickname, an ironic reference to a cook and maid in *To Kill a Mockingbird*, since everybody complained about my lackadaisical work ethic and lack of subservience.

"Calpurnia, do you have my *People* magazine?" one of the annoyed agents would scream.

"I'm almost done," I'd explain, refusing to part with the trades or gossip rags until I was finished.

This was my real introduction to show business, which not only excused eccentric behavior but seemed to reward it. The agency dealt with difficult clients, studio heads, managers, and executives, so my sassy black girl behavior didn't faze them one bit. It amused them and broke up the monotony of the work.

In retrospect I see I had a perpetual fear of consistency, of settling into a job, working hard, and looking up thirty years later only to find myself still there. While I didn't want to get fired, because I needed the job, I also didn't want to get promoted and have a reason to stay too long.

My claustrophobia wasn't reserved only for my relationships; it would descend upon me at the earliest signs of stability

in most areas of my life. You'd think that an unstable upbringing would have me fighting to establish a secure future, but it
didn't. That was the road my sister Renee had taken with her
job for the state of New York. That kind of average, workaday
job was not how I envisioned my future. I craved a life different
than the grind of necessity—different than the jobs I watched
adults work growing up. To me this job was a stopgap measure,
and I intended to keep it that way.

I was so busy throwing myself into my new California life
that I didn't bother to find a therapist or to deal with my abandonment issues. I convinced myself that a change of scenery
was all I needed to be happy. I also discovered that the best way
to get over an ex was to get involved with the next man.

Clean came to Los Angeles to work and introduced me to more
of his friends. Barry had been a child actor who made the transition to adult actor while never losing his boyish charm or need
for attention. I would later understand that many actors suffer
from Peter Pan syndrome, staying in an arrested-development
phase longer than anyone might imagine possible. Child actors
tend to have people constantly hovering, taking care of their
most basic needs, finding housing, paying bills, shopping for
gifts, etc. A team of people is always in place to ensure that an
actor doesn't have the slightest discomfort. Actors are allowed
to be different, and people cater to those differences. Barry had
a host of people who took care of things that he didn't want to,
including canceling things he had committed to do—not to
mention the constant crowd of women and fans fawning over
the actor like he was a newborn baby whose poop still smelled
like syrup.

Barry showed up at the Gage Group regularly, always
claiming to be in the neighborhood. He flirted, asking me out
while at the same time explaining his allegiance to Clean.

"I can't mess with you, girl," he'd insist, even though he was the one showing up at my job.

Because Barry worked all the time and was successful, nobody complained about him showing up. The agents were always ready to pounce on any opening to steal Barry away from his representation.

At the same time Spike Lee, a good friend from New York, came to Los Angeles to premier *She's Gotta Have It*. Spike became an overnight success, and since I had a small part in the movie, some of that glitter sprinkled onto me. Spike always showed up at the Gage Group to visit, and nobody minded our two-hour lunches talking smack and celebrating his success and the insanely large picture he saw for himself.

At some point Barry wore me down with his persistence, and I fell head over heels; although he wasn't my type, he could make me laugh and make me feel protected, but mostly he helped me forget about Gary. Barry also chauffeured me around, fed me, and made me feel cared for.

Unfortunately for me, Barry needed constant validation, especially by women—lots of women—to prove his worth. His success as an actor had women constantly propositioning him for sex. Like Chris Rock joked, "Men are only as faithful as their options," and Barry had lots of options. He could not be faithful to save his life, but I naively assumed that Barry would outgrow his need to sleep around.

After I'd catch Barry smelling of another woman and threaten to leave him, he'd turn on the crocodile tears, pleading, "Baby, please, she didn't mean anything to me. Don't allow some woman to ruin us."

"No woman forced you to stick your thing in her, so don't blame no woman," I'd rage.

Barry was smooth enough to change course, always jabbing at my Achilles heel. "I love you more than I ever loved another woman. I need you. Please, I'll change—just give me another chance."

I knew he had some growing up to do, but I also believed he loved me and that mattered most of all. I tried not to take his flaws personally and attributed his dog-in-heat activities to simple immaturity. Throughout history men had changed for the love of a great woman, and that's what I expected from Barry.

It took a long time to learn that Barry was incapable of changing his spots, love or no love. On Valentine's Day two years later, as Barry celebrated Mardi Gras with friends in New Orleans, I packed my belongings and moved back to my aunt's house.

After the breakup with Barry, I suffered a minor breakdown, lost weight, couldn't eat or sleep, and cried nonstop, although somehow I managed to hold on to a nine-to-five. At this point in my life the distraction of a relationship had a positive effect on my body and food issues. I was a size 4 and easily maintained the weight by eating normally and working out. But once Barry and I broke up, I went into a depression, became anxious, and couldn't remember to eat. I could go days without eating, and my weight dropped down to about a hundred pounds. With my five-foot-five-inch frame I looked sickly.

A friend, seeing me broken and barely functional, offered a spiritual solution—the Self-Realization Fellowship Lake Shrine in Pacific Palisades, a beautiful, calming sanctuary surrounded by gardens, the lake itself filled with koi, ducks, swans, and lotus flowers. At first skeptical that anything could transform me back into a normal human being, I was soon proven wrong. Entering the gates of this peaceful oasis, I was surprised by its effect: I felt like I could breathe for the first time since my breakup.

I started driving to the Lake Shrine a few times a week to sit with myself, something I had never done before. This was different from the silence in the long corridor outside my childhood bedroom where the doors to my mother's and sisters' rooms were closed. This whole entree into spiritual searching was new to me. In my experience, silent alone time had been a form of punishment, reminding me of my childhood. My mother couldn't handle the noise of children, so most nights we'd all go in our rooms to read, daydream, write, or whatever we could do to keep off her nerves. Since childhood, too much silence filled me with sadness, a feeling of hopelessness, and the desire for the distraction of noise.

I had purposely surrounded myself with friends, focusing on gossip and men instead of myself. I was not sure if I loved myself or didn't love myself, but I was not about to risk finding out by getting to know myself.

The friend who first took me to the Lake Shrine also introduced me to other ideas that I never would have found on my own—inward-looking solutions to problems, like meditation, the books of Florence Scovel Shinn, even the Hollywood Church of Religious Science. Her successful, calm life was a testament to her spiritual beliefs, and I truly wanted her kind of self-esteem; I just didn't know how to make that transition from where I was standing. Nothing and no one in my past had ever suggested taking an inner look, fixing myself from the inside out.

As I started learning meditation and seeking spiritual guidance, I couldn't shake the gnawing feeling that I was truly an awful, unlovable person, that the reason I was molested was because my uncle saw straight to my core, that I was worthless and deserved to be abused and abandoned. I feared that I was different from other women who were worthy of love and support, and nothing I did or said would ever change this.

The more work I did on myself, the more anxiety I had, because of deep-seated beliefs I held about myself. Always when I got close to these feelings, I would distract myself with a friend or a boyfriend or some minor crisis.

I would do anything to avoid taking an honest look at myself.

What Goes Down
Must Come Up

Like I said, I left Barry on Valentine's Day. The date had everything to do with getting his attention and making a valid point. His going on vacation with six guys was not the appropriate thing to do over the most romantic day of the year, which was only the icing on the burned, falling-down cake that was our relationship. I left him not because I wanted to, but because I had grown tired of all the influence people had on him and of his inability to simply grow up. I had put up with so much while I was with Barry, all because I believed our love would outlast his need to validate himself with other women. He wasn't alone in being juvenile. I regularly caused drama and big scenes, throwing tantrums, slamming out of cars on the side of busy highways, behavior I hoped would end before my twenty-fifth birthday.

I had been working for Barry's manager, and when I quit Barry, I quit her too. My hippie childhood of running off when things got tough did not prepare me to sit through uncomfortable emotional states. Especially ones that would require me to field telephone calls from my ex-lover on a daily basis. My impulsive need to wipe the slate clean of people cost me a few great relationships in my life, but for a long time I didn't know how to be any other way.

I started taking a commercial acting class, hoping to make enough money in television to afford me the luxury to stay home and write the rest of the time. Kelly, a spunky blond Canadian, approached me on the first day of class. Her straightforward manner and no-bull attitude made us fast friends. Like a couple of clucking hens we sat back and snidely passed judgment on the parade of Hollywood wannabe stars and starlets performing circus tricks for the teacher, a has-been commercial king who reigned supreme in his day. He strutted his Pillsbury Doughboy body across the stage, explaining how if we were ever lucky enough to become him we'd have made it in Hollywood. Neither Kelly nor I was new to the spoils of Hollywood, so unlike the newbies swarming for his attention we both remained skeptical about his power to transform us into imitations of himself. Luckily for the teacher, he had the forethought to channel a once-lucrative career into a dream to dangle over those of us who had yet to get our turn at the silver screen or television screen or whatever. Kelly and I quickly realized neither of us had the aptitude or ability to brown-nose enough to win that coveted slot of teacher's pet, so instead we spent our time taking pot shots at people's hair or diction or anything else that would make us feel superior.

We didn't like the break-you-down-to-build-you-up technique the teacher and so many others in Hollywood were adept at using, manipulating fame seekers into believing the teachers were responsible for whatever success their students had. By the third class Kelly and I were apartment hunting, discussing the benefits of being roommates.

Don't get me wrong—we weren't behaving like bratty dilettantes. It's just that once we realized the only way to get on the teacher's good side was to ogle and compliment him on his national Tide commercials, we settled on sitting in the back of the classroom and having fun.

Within a month we had moved into an apartment complex on the corner of Hollywood Boulevard and Laurel Canyon, an intersection of typical Los Angeles traffic and smog. Laurel Canyon is a road leading to ex-hippie hangouts that have now been turned into four-bedroom homes for celebrities and Hollywood executives. Living at the bottom, I became aware of the large number of successful people driving past on their way up the hill to their luxurious homes.

Flaming Colossus, the hot-spot club where Kelly worked on weekends, became my second job. Kelly had the unique ability to make the most of any meeting. It never occurred to her to try her luck waiting tables at IHOP; she always managed to find employment at the hottest restaurant or club of the moment.

Our work dress code was hip, black, and the skimpier the better. Mega movie and rock stars frequented the Colossus, as Kelly and I flew around in our barely there wear, balancing trays of overpriced drinks. While I'd hang out for an occasional drink after work, Kelly always stayed and partied with the owners and other employees, never getting home until hours later.

After a wild night of boozing it up, Kelly would often wake me up blasting Patsy Cline's "Crazy" at the highest volume. It's a wonder none of the neighbors complained about Kelly's 4:00 a.m. ritual. If you are depressed, Patsy Cline can send you right over the edge, and even though I have no proof, I'm sure plenty of suicide notes were written while listening to her music. I'd wake, half-dressed, in a bad mood, and stumble into the living room, where I'd find Kelly smoking a cigarette, glass of wine in hand, swaying to Patsy with a huge drunken smile plastered on her face. She'd wrap her skinny arms around my neck, oblivious to my sour disposition in that way the inebriated have of expecting you to join their party. "Hey baby doll," she'd greet me, as if I had somehow welcomed this opportunity to party, and she'd drunkenly attempt a dance.

As much as Kelly's nocturnal activities pissed me off, right there below my surface annoyance I knew exactly how she felt. Nothing was lonelier than the hours I spent slinging drinks for happy couples, singles ready to mingle, and the alcoholics and addicts who drowned their sorrows in frothy mugs on my shift. It made me painfully aware of how alone I felt in the world. Having a sister who used drugs and alcohol to the point that employment was never a possibility, I found drunkenness to be a real turn-off. I remembered the drunken women wandering around my neighborhood as a kid. Although I'd see way more men in a drunken stupor, there was something about women stumbling around in this state that disgusted me. It seemed unnatural that a woman would think so little of herself.

I had vowed early in life that I would never allow myself to fall so far into a bottle that the sight of me would cause disgust. Having others see me looking raggedy was more than my fragile ego could handle. The last thing I ever wanted was to be one of those women who randomly lose control in public. The idea of people pointing and passing judgment brought back memories of my childhood, my self-consciousness when people smirked at my worn shoes and hand-me-down clothing. I always took extra precautions not to stray too far from the appearance of an acceptable normal.

The shame of being overweight would have felt like another version of my worst childhood memories. It would have shown the world that I was not special or even normal but an out-of-control eater who deserved to be humiliated. So I began to feel an intense pressure to be thin, which was difficult since my weight was closer to average. Slowly I was becoming consumed by thoughts of both. When a friend's teenage daughter came over I measured her thighs with my hands, trying to see how much larger I was than her. Placing my thumbs together,

I'd attempt to make my forefingers touch. I wanted to be that kind of thin.

Just as Kelly would drown her sorrows in drink, I'd stuff down my feelings with food. I depended on food to make me feel better when things had gone wrong or to take the edge off a bad day. So it made sense that I would develop a passion for cooking, which allowed me a place to put all my anxiety while doing something creative. Making meals for Kelly and my friends became my way of building a family outside of my own. I had an open-door policy, and friends knew that they could always drop by for a meal. But because I tended to make rich, heavy Southern dinners I'd find my weight creeping up, sending me off in search of the latest diet. I didn't seem able to give up eating rich foods for long, so keeping the extra pounds off seemed impossible. Because I was now auditioning for television commercials, a few extra pounds became more of a big deal.

Kelly was a happy drunk but would drink far past the point of pretty. I never gave her any flak about her alcohol consumption, especially knowing I had secrets of my own. As roommates go, she maintained a good job and could always sway me out of a funk. When I had a breakup, Kelly sent me not only flowers but also a note: "Time wounds all heels." I kept that note for years. Whether it was a breakup, heartbreak over some man I chose who didn't choose me, or even pain in the realization that I pushed away good men who chose me, Kelly helped make everything better.

It was impossible not to recognize my mother in myself, especially when it came to men. Instead of being the open, gullible heart waiting for its other half, like the words inscribed on a Hallmark card, I gave up on love. After the disappointment of Barry, I discovered I had resumed my mother's need to flee at the sight, taste, touch, feel, and smell of love. The thought of love and loving overwhelmed me. I'd ask myself, *How many times do you have to fail at something to learn that maybe it isn't for you in this lifetime?*

Denying myself the option of loving hurt so much, but I took a masochistic pleasure in that kind of pain. If I started to like someone, I'd scold myself with reminders that I was unlikable and that no one could love me. I told myself that once a man saw how damaged I really was, he would abandon me, just as my father had, and I would be worse off than I was without love.

As much as it hurt, it fueled something in me. I began to write again, stories of loss and remorse and women who had left their hearts open only to discover the brutality awaiting them. Opening my heart even a crack felt paralyzing. Yes, it scares a lot of people, even people I know, but they didn't all react the way I did. They don't run screaming in the opposite direction and, if that doesn't work, they don't take two massively strong arms and (metaphorically) shove the person away before he knows what hit him. The girl/woman who had always held out the hope that one day a man would love her now refused any hint of that hope at all. But though I appeared guarded and suspicious on the surface, below it I wanted to be loved more than anything. More than I wanted to be skinny or rich or popular.

But no matter how I tried, whenever I met a guy I liked I could never successfully convey my true feelings to him. Years later I'd run into men from my past, and they'd always tell me how into me they were at the time, but I wouldn't let them get close. I had been so worried about getting my own heart broken that most of the time I was the one doing the damage to them.

And when I got weak to the need for love, I only chose those whose love could never overwhelm me, those whose love didn't make me feel vulnerable. They were the ones who didn't arouse any passion and who would always love me more than I loved them. I needed to be in control. I wanted power over my emotions, and I didn't care how I got it.

As I withdrew emotionally, I focused on what I felt I could control: my career. I got an agent and hit the pavement, auditioning for film, television, and commercials. I would get close, but rarely would I get the job. I started hanging out with actresses and models; suddenly my size 4/5 with black-girl curves seemed large compared with my biracial and black girlfriends who had long since released any physical references to booty-licious, staying a size 2 or even 0. Now, next to these new friends, I was heavy. They all knew that the camera added ten pounds, but when I looked in the mirror I saw twenty or thirty extra pounds. I developed what I would later learn is called body dysmorphic disorder. Put simply, I saw my body differently than it really was.

I had dieted before, trying and failing with every diet and quick fix that promised you'd lose ten pounds in ten days. For the first time since I moved from New York, where I'd started taking diuretics and diet pills and was ten pounds heavier, I was having real problems with my body again. Those ten pounds that I had lost once I moved to California came back.

My issues with men and food began to blend, causing one gigantic internal nightmare. I peacocked, puffing out my chest and bragging about how I liked to be independent and single, how I hungered for simplicity. But in fact love was the only thing I craved.

And so I ate. Instead of admitting to myself how desperately I craved love, which I saw as weak, I pushed down my needs for companionship, intimacy, and affection and smothered them with food. I began to back away from my friends. I also discovered that I was incapable of quitting men cold turkey. If I felt the slightest pangs of loneliness or sadness, anxiety, or self-loathing I would reach for food. It had the immediate power to calm whatever was bothering me. When I was stuffed, it proved harder to access feelings of fear or rage or sorrow. I stopped depending on the comfort of lovers or friends, instead choosing to smash down any uncomfortable emotions with sugar or starch. I wasn't aware that food had become my lover, my friend. I only knew that if I ate something I would no longer feel anything . . . except full.

It was easy to fool myself into thinking that I really didn't need anything or anyone as long as I had something else to cling to. And when I ate too much I could exercise like a fiend to exorcise the extra pounds I had put on. And because I looked normal, I convinced myself that nothing was wrong with this new way of functioning. Eating didn't always stop the need for strong arms holding me, but temporarily it made me forget how strong that need had become.

Occasionally I'd meet a new guy, a possibility, but if he was available, I always found some reason to shoot him down. Always I sabotaged burgeoning relationships or picked men who were as unavailable as I had become. It was so much easier to focus on men who were not there for me emotionally, physically, or mentally than it was to see the common denominator of these bad choices: ME. So I sold myself on this self-fulfilling prophecy that men and I didn't mix.

I wanted to be absent in my body, to feel nothing, and I didn't know how to get there because I hurt all the time. I drifted farther and farther away from any connection to my feelings, teetering on the edge of an alternate reality, unable to see things as they really were.

I felt as hopeless after not getting a call back for an audition as I did when a guy didn't call me after a date. It didn't matter if I wanted the second date or not; I wanted to be the one to control the temperature of a relationship. I should be the one to reject, devastate, maim. Every disappointment dragged me back into the past of abandonment, sexual abuse, and acute awareness of what my life lacked.

Auditioning pushed me over the edge of my frail sanity. Parading in front of a panel of casting directors, producers, a director, and assistants poised to pass judgment not only on my performance but on me destroyed me. Measuring myself through their prying eyes, I always found myself lacking, perhaps not always at that moment but definitely by the time that call came from my agent saying, "You didn't get the role."

I wasn't yet aware that I hated acting. I only knew that most of my friends wanted desperately to perform, and I liked the lifestyle. I liked not having to punch a clock or to take jobs that dampened my dreams. My father hated his chosen profession of accounting but did it because it provided financial stability. Acting seemed like the lesser of two evils. I could work only occasionally and still afford to live a lifestyle similar to someone who slaved away full-time. More than anything I craved freedom, and naively I believed acting would provide that for me.

And with every rejection came a little more unhappiness with myself. Instead of being a confident, creative, twenty-something professional, living out the dream of auditioning for roles in the film capital of the world, I went reeling back to my grade-school self, back to a time when I never measured up, when I was always hungry, starving for food, attention, and, mostly, love. To that faceless group of judges sitting before me, I was just one in a long line of nameless actresses vying for a role. But the procedure unbalanced me. I did not view the audition process as a means to an end; rather I viewed their approval as essential to validate that I mattered as a person and that I was in fact somebody who could be loved. But that validation rarely happened. After each audition, I felt hollow, empty, and hungry for something to fill the hole of rejection by others and my rejection of myself. So I would come home and eat.

It didn't matter that I already felt a size or two too large for whatever role I competed for. I reached for comfort—cold, hot, sweet, salty, fried, baked. I wanted something to transport me away from these feelings of dissatisfaction with myself. And even though the comfort was only temporary, food—something that, like love, I never had enough of as a child—seemed to be the salve I needed for my relentless internal wounds.

But like that seemingly perfect lover who turns on you when you least expect his betrayal, food began to invite its own problems into my life. I could no longer control my consumption, nor could I work off the quantities I ate during my binges. My internal dissatisfaction and self-hate began to manifest themselves physically, showing on my body, there for everyone to see, and I felt ashamed. My thighs began to grow into Vs, bulging both at the inner and outer thigh. My body stretched my clothing past the point of comfort.

One day around this time, I sat in my apartment reading some chick magazine, enviously eyeing the fashions on the superthin supermodels, when an article caught my eye: "Bulimia, the New Diet." A normal person reading this exposé about the dangers of bulimia would have been jarred or disgusted by the practices of this disease. But for someone in my fragile mental state, in need of control, the inclusion of that word "diet" made this is an educational how-to. I was off and running, desperate for this miracle diet to work its magic.

But it took some practice. I shoved my fingers down my throat, jerking them toward the back of my tonsils, for weeks before I could successfully throw up. Years later, I got sick for real and threw up for the first time without trying, and finally I understood why people blanched in horror at the thought of someone vomiting on purpose. The two acts are entirely different. Bulimia provides a warm, calming feeling that's soothing, while throwing up involuntarily felt violent and painful. The first time I convinced my body to eject its contents, I was terrified. Yet immediately afterward I felt more relaxed than I had in ages, as if a huge weight had been lifted from me. That feeling of anxiety that constantly sat at the pit of my stomach disappeared. I could eat whatever I wanted and never gain weight. And most important, no one would ever see how broken I was inside.

To me, this bulimia was magic. I noticed people beginning to compliment me on my weight loss. I loved being referred to as skinny. The words *You are so skinny* became a high for me. I lived to hear them. Before long I had dropped down to a size 2. I felt free, powerful, invincible, and perfect.

While my dress size decreased, I went from zero to a thousand on the addict scale. After a few short months on the bulimia train, I couldn't stop myself. At first I purged once in a while, only after I had eaten large quantities of fatty food, but it progressed to a daily need for the calm that came afterward. If someone hurt my feelings or I experienced fear or disappointment, I'd find myself in the midst of a binge before I could stop, knowing the purge would follow.

I lost control, no longer able to choose when, where, or even if I would binge and purge. I was quickly caught up in the grasp of this bulimic hell, doing it day and night, and nothing could free me of its hold on my life.

I tried to talk myself into starving by making deals: "If you don't eat all day long, you can have a big binge at night."

All my emotions, fears, and insecurities would well up to the surface, and before I could stop myself I'd be off and running to the nearest grocery store, doughnut shop, or mini-mart. Stumbling out of the car with my purchases, my mouth stuffed with muffins, cupcakes, or some other sugary, doughy treat, I'd rush into the apartment to get my binge on. An hour would pass as I stuffed myself full of food, trying to squash down and ignore feelings of shame. Eventually I'd find my way to the toilet to purge two or three times until I was certain no food remained inside me.

I'd tell myself I didn't deserve to eat. Returning to the scene of the crime, I'd stuff the remaining food deep down into the garbage, covering items with newspapers or whatever else I could find to avoid any evidence that could lead to questions about my behavior. Usually an hour would pass before I got that panicked, starving urge again. It gripped me like a physical ache, propelling me to do it once more. I was incapable of stopping myself. I'd dig down in the garbage for the discarded leftovers. I always threw food away in its package, as if I knew I'd return to fish it out, digging past the potato peels and empty milk cartons. Then I'd start consuming tons of calories in an effort to stuff down more feelings of shame and unworthiness. Sometimes I'd finish a binge and then get the urge a third or fourth time and have to drive to another grocery store farther away, afraid a store clerk would notice me, to get more food to continue bingeing. After a while I'd fall asleep from the sheer exhaustion of throwing up my guts. My jaws and throat would ache from the steady abuse, but I was powerless to stop.

I had to be supercareful in case Kelly came home and found me in midbinge, which did occur on occasion. I'd play it off like I was high and having the munchies. It was better to confess to pot use than an eating disorder. I would have confessed to a lot of things as long as it would keep people from knowing my secret shame. Then I'd lock myself in the bathroom, run the water to pretend I was taking a shower, and proceed to throw up for fifteen or twenty minutes.

My face started to look like it had swollen after being beaten to a pulp. Instead of my angular West Indian bone structure, I developed chipmunk cheeks that protruded off the sides of my face. I had bags and dark circles under my eyes where blood vessels began to burst. I was becoming less myself and more a stranger whose body had been invaded by this disease, but there was nothing I could do to stop.

Bulimia became such a big part of my life that I altered my lifestyle to accommodate it. I found it increasingly difficult to binge and purge with Kelly always coming and going unannounced, catching me in some stage of my ritual abuse. As soon as a one-bedroom apartment opened in our complex, I explained away my need to live alone and scooted over to my solitary apartment. I wanted a place where I would be free to act out my disorder without any prying eyes or well-meaning roommate trying to figure out why I was eating a dozen pancakes followed by doughnuts and muffins and a long list of other things I ate to keep fear at bay.

In a short time, I had become a professional bulimic, practicing my behavior day and night, shutting out all people and events that did not include food. I would close the blinds and spend hours upon hours bingeing and purging. I thought about food 24-7, whether I wanted to or not. Life became about getting food, avoiding food, starving, overeating, exercising, downing laxatives, and purging around the clock.

Once I came of age and could choose my own friends, I substituted those relationships for the close family ties that I refused to have. I never made a conscious decision to replace my family; I was way too separated from my emotions to be that Machiavellian. But I hadn't connected with my relatives in any real or meaningful way in a long time.

Even Felicia and I had parted company; she stayed true to her childhood dreams and married straight out of high school, having two children by the age of twenty. For a while we tried staying close, but a complete lack of interest in the life the other chose made it impossible to merge over anything but a shared past, and neither of us wanted to live in those memories anymore. My mother and my sisters were busy with their own lives, or so I told myself.

The bigger truth had to do with the shame of being from a poor family. I believed that if I stayed too close, I would wind up trapped in the cycle of poverty like my mother and grandmother. I desperately set out to re-create myself in an image of my own making, one that didn't necessary meld with the harsher, truer reality. I rarely talked about my childhood except in sweeping bullet points. I needed to be something other than the daughter of a gypsy or the sister of a junkie or the sister of an abused wife or the abandoned daughter of a successful, narcissistic father. I wanted to be me, whoever that was, without any labels Velcroed to my backside and without feeling subjected to a lifetime of limitations.

But once I adopted bulimia, my friendships became transient. I avoided people who knew me in favor of strangers who believed whatever version of my life I chose to tell. Gone were the East Coast intellectuals and fellow struggling artists I'd known for a few years, traded in for the narcissistic gym instructor who could show me how to sculpt perfect abs or the up-and-coming movie actress who couldn't string together a sentence that wasn't about her, because they never minded paying the restaurant bill for our meals. There was a steady succession of new "best" friends. I became a professional listener and support person, doling out advice on dieting, dating, and careers, even as my own life was being held together by lies and tape. I kept these new friends and old friends far apart, always fearing they would exchange and compare creatively spun versions of my messy life. I barely managed to get any writing done and spent my free time manipulating people into feeding me. Because of my growing obsession with all things food, I couldn't get through a day without falling mouth first into some eating. I was barely able to hold on to a job because the bingeing was so disruptive so I began to bargain with myself, raising the bar every hour if that's what it took to keep me from taking that first bite. *You can binge on more expensive food, or you can drive farther to get a favorite binge food.*

Of course, I couldn't have food in my stomach. I would be seized by great anxiety over finding myself stuck with anything except air and water inside my body. After eating even the smallest portions of food, I would feel a cross between calm and an anxiety attack coming on. I'd excuse myself from gatherings, restaurants, dinner parties, my friends, my dates, in order to seek a safe refuge to purge. Like a heroin addict, after every session I grew anxious trying to figure out how to get the next binge and purge started.

I became aware of the racism surrounding my disease: Because I was a black girl with natural hair who had grown up below the poverty line, no one ever suspected I could be bulimic. Maybe it wasn't racism as much as a simple ignorance that melanin content did not guarantee me an eating-disorder-free life. My color became the perfect shield against suspicion. No one questioned why I ate three or four helpings per meal, why food went missing, why I never had any money or motivation, and why I never gained weight. I learned a lot about bulimics both from reading and by observing them. We are not like anorexics, who are more reserved, avoiding the spotlight as if they are waiting for permission to grab it. Now it's only my observation, but I've noticed that bulimics are outgoing perfectionists who can be bubbly and helpful, deflecting from the deeper truth of isolation, fear, and shame.

For a while I had everyone fooled—until I got a job waiting tables at Butterfield's restaurant on Sunset Boulevard. Butterfield's was as famous for its Sunday brunch as it was for being the former home of Hollywood lothario John Barrymore. On Sundays, the wait station was weighted down with baked goods in anticipation of the hungry crowds. Waiters filled bread baskets with croissants, muffins, brioche, sweet rolls, and other flour- and sugar-based treats.

During my first few months working there, I had successfully maneuvered around the gaping jaws of my bulimia by refusing to take that first bite at work. Try as I might, I could never take a first bite without it leading to a fateful second and a third and so on until I wound up puking out my guts into the toilet in a daze. I knew how it worked, so somehow I managed to hold on to control most of the time. But I couldn't stave off the bulimia forever.

One Sunday morning I slipped that first sweet bite into my mouth. Everything became a blur; the customers, the food orders, Bloody Marys, mimosas, and cocktails were all left waiting as I shoveled the sweet breads down my throat. I wanted—no, I needed—to disappear into the food, to quell the loud sound of shame with each and every bite. Ignoring my customers I kept running into the single-stall bathroom to toss up the food before heading back to the nearest breadbasket to begin again. Until a male waiter caught me midbinge and gave me a severe look of disapproval.

"Girl, you need to stop going in that bathroom throwing up and take care of your customers."

All the other waiters turned in my direction, their expressions one gigantic "amen" meant to silence any denial on my part. My secret was no longer a secret. Blinded by the bright light of discovery, I finished my shift, fighting to control my anxiety, refusing to take another bite. When my shift ended, I scurried out of there like a drowned rat in need of a blow dryer, certain that I would never return. My deepest, darkest secret had been exposed. I couldn't go on pretending I was normal, and I resigned. I was so bad at the job, I left only moments before the manager would have gotten around to firing me anyway.

This was not the first job I'd quit or lose due to my disease, but it was the first time I'd been exposed to ridicule due to my little habit of throwing up. I vowed to be more careful. The exposure was unbearable, and I didn't know how I'd survive the next time.

In most areas of my life I had always come last. In birth order, I was my mother's final child. I was the last of my friends to sprout breasts and to menstruate, the absolute signal that womanhood had begun. I was the last among my peers to lose my virginity. And now, even when it came to bulimia, I would later discover that most bulimics had a ten-year head start, having begun the practice in their early teens. But even though I started bulimia in my early twenties I was a quick study, and I effortlessly caught up, even surpassing those who had begun their addiction earlier.

Manorexic

My bulimic behavior made it impossible for me to stay focused enough to take care of myself. So, like a broken record, I again gave up my apartment, although the landlord would use different words to describe the ending of our business arrangement. I put all my worldly goods in storage, and I crawled back to my aunt's townhouse in Pasadena. Her home often served as a way station where I retreated between the bruised chapters of my life story.

I blamed my descent into my bulimic nightmare on my isolation and living alone, and so I sought out my aunt's home, hoping her companionship would be at least a temporary solution that would force me to stop bingeing and throwing up. My aunt worked for the city on women's issues and was a major player in numerous organizations, so I knew she was up on all things female and could bust me in my addictive behavior. If there was one thing that I hoped could temporarily pause my addiction, it was the threat of discovery.

So for a while I was able to shove my addiction aside, choosing instead to worship its faithful companion, anorexia.

Unlike bulimia, which left me feeling drained of everything but self-loathing, anorexia made me feel superior and untouchable. Anorexia made me feel like I was floating in a cloud high above the mere mortals gobbling down ridiculous amounts of calories because of a basic lack of control. I experienced this internal high, along with smugness, whenever I was able to avoid a meal or to eat only one kind of low-calorie food in small portions for days. On the days when I ate more than I believed I should, I would berate myself, raising the bar higher and higher in order to survive on as little as possible. But eventually I failed at anorexia and had to take that first bite that made me delve back into bulimia. That is, until a better distraction came along.

When it came to a new man entering my life, I gobbled down love like a greedy child left alone with a bag full of Halloween candy. And like that child, I'd eventually be left with a sour feeling in the pit of my stomach and a hunger for something more satisfying. My friend Don once accused me of being gullible when it came to men. Just the fact that some man I'd deemed worthy felt the same desire to shower his attention onto me always sent my heart fluttering. Attention and compliments meant more to me than sincerity or commitment because I didn't know the difference. And like that greedy kid, I gobbled up all the attention and could become insatiable for that man until . . . I had him. Then I'd turn into a boxed-in rodent, running in circles, bumping into walls to flee the confines of that small space, a man's heart.

Acting in a television movie in South Central Los Angeles, I met Jonathan, a rare white face among the throngs of blacks on the inner-city production. He zeroed in on me. I had always been an easy mark for a man who knew what he wanted, especially when it was me. Something about swirling at the center of a man's universe made me feel important, worthy, and finally valued, but then what woman wouldn't? If I found a man smart and funny I'd usually allow myself to fall for him. It wouldn't matter if he was fat or handsome, rich or poor, old or young—intelligence trumped everything, including good common sense.

Jonathan was my white knight, tall, moderately handsome, funny, smart, self-effacing, and cocky. And he wanted me, not in the temporary get-naked-on-the-sofa, go-home-in-the-middle-of-the-night-and-pretend-it-never-happened way. Or even in the I-want-to-chase-you-till-I-have-you-then-you'll-see-how-messed-up-and-unavailable-I-am kind of way. He seemed to be the real deal, single, successful, and unafraid of commitment.

Our relationship started casually enough. Jonathan would stand around with a bunch of the crew guys telling war stories, always in an effort to get my attention, and one day he finally did. He would rush to sit next to me at lunch, and he always saved a place for me at breakfast.

Of course, I was too busy being fawned over to notice that Jonathan rarely ate, always choosing caffeine and nicotine over any real sustenance. I, on the other hand, pretended to be normal, shoving average-sized portions into my mouth and keeping them down because I was already filled up on Jonathan's undivided attention. Everything I did and said was fascinating to him, and he ate my charm with a spoon. I thought his anxiety about seeing his first writing project produced was affecting his normal appetite so I never made too big a deal over his eating. I didn't realize that not eating was normal for him.

I was also unaware that it was my dark chocolate skin that sealed the deal. Jonathan had a massive case of jungle fever, the darker the berry and all that. Several years later he would get his wish by marrying a black woman.

Within a week Jonathan and I were as close to being a couple as I could allow myself. For hours into the night we talked about our desires and dreams for that perfect loving family.

"I want five sons," Jonathan bragged, "so that they can be the UCLA basketball team's starting lineup."

Magically we wanted all the same things out of life—he, a wife and family to take care of, and I, a loving husband to take care of me. We were simpatico. Since I was between apartments and had been living far out in Pasadena with my aunt, on our official first date he gave me his other garage-door opener. Of course, the garage-door opener had been attached to the car of his fiancée only a week earlier, but as far as I was concerned we had a real connection, and nothing, not even basic common sense, could infringe upon our path to bliss. Conveniently, he also had a set of house keys lying around that were passed on to me.

I felt high knowing that Jonathan had chosen me over his ex, but had I been more self-aware I would have been able to track this directly to my father and the simple fact that he never once chose me over anything or anyone. My elation was similar to that I felt when I starved myself of food. Jonathan and this relationship became my substitute drug.

I transferred my belongings from a suitcase into a set of drawers at Jonathan's and quickly made myself at home. Caught up in the excitement of this new love, I turned my passion away from food and focused on Jonathan. Finally, I had found the cure, the solution for all my food problems: love. I took the bare refrigerator and cabinets as further testament to Jonathan's needing me to rescue him from bachelorhood. I daydreamed of solidifying our union over morning breakfasts and nightly dinners.

But eventually Jonathan's aversion to food toppled all my white-picket-fence, home-cooked-meal fantasies. In my version the man was thrilled to have a woman who lovingly slaved over the stove in order to provide him with proper sustenance before he went out in the world to slay dragons and bring home the bacon, preferably the applewood-smoked kind.

Jonathan confessed that he wasn't a big eater. What frequency had I been vibrating on the past few weeks? How did I miss that? When I explained to Jonathan that I intended to actually cook meals in his kitchen, he seemed excited but nervous. I attributed his hesitancy to the fact that I was asking for credit cards to buy necessities, things like pots, pans, and spatulas, the works. Cheap could send me packing quicker than anything, 'cause, even though I hadn't ever been able to go gold digga on a man, I expected generosity.

I should have run when he started explaining his "simple" tastes for skinless baked, broiled, or grilled chicken with steamed vegetables and the occasional inclusion of brown rice. To a girl who grew up forced to eat whatever travesty was plopped onto her plate at night and called dinner, this was insane. Food, even before my bulimia had taken on a larger-than-life role, needed to be dressed up, seasoned properly, and shared with those lucky enough to not have had my childhood.

In an effort to rewrite history, or to at least create it, I wanted to give myself the dinnertime ritual I'd never had. That meant starting with a tasty, flavorful meal someone (me) had prepared and presenting it to someone (him) who enjoyed eating. I tried to introduce Jonathan to breakfast, Southern style—pork sausage, omelets, home fries, and biscuits. Can we discuss the fact that in this day and age I chose to make him home-made buttermilk biscuits instead of the straight-out-the-can version, which were a huge treat in my childhood?

My first meal was a total disaster, with me trying to seduce him with food in the same way that most women use sex to get a man's attention. How dare he butcher my Betty Crocker dreams? But Jonathan was immune to the joys of home cooking. He reached again and again for caffeine and nicotine, explaining his sensitive digestive tract and how he'd suffer if he ate the kinds of food I cooked.

"Try it," I prodded unsuccessfully.

My next meal was as close as I could come to his suggestion that I forgo any oil or fat, a chicken stir-fry in a spicy sauce.

"Did you cook that in oil?" He blanched, looking more than a little horrified. "Can you use that nonfat cooking spray or low-fat broth?" he'd press.

As I chopped ginger and garlic, Jonathan wandered into the kitchen yet again, this time standing over my shoulder to get a better view of the pan. "Are you going to sauté those vegetables? Because I have a steamer . . ." This went on until he had dismissed everything that could be construed as tasty or appetizing.

Still, I attributed this to Jonathan's being a health nut, the kind they warn you about at the local airport when you land. Granola liberals, I'd heard men called when it came to the nuts-and-twigs variety of the male species indigenous to the West Coast. But Jonathan didn't quite fit the mold with his propensity to chain smoke and drink unlimited cups of coffee with nonfat milk.

And for a while, floating in that pink love bubble, I couldn't see the correlation between his relationship to food and mine. That could have been due to his other vice—talking. He loved the sound of his own voice, each syllable, and spewed out his every thought. Nothing I did could convince him to use that mouth for the more life-affirming necessity of eating. For a couple weeks I plied Jonathan with food cooked in small amounts of butter or oil, which he'd notice as soon as he took one bite, then refuse to take another, always with an excuse meant to distract me from his issues with food.

He practiced behaviors that, had I been less self-obsessed, would have been large red flags. While I would eat a meal, Jonathan would down large glasses of ice water, always excited about the effect on his empty stomach.

"I love feeling the water work its way down my throat," he'd laugh. "Don't you enjoy when your stomach is empty and the ice tingles your insides?"

For me, this brought up feelings of self-disgust and self-loathing about the fact that I couldn't get more control over my eating. Note to self: no woman wants to be with a man who eats less than she does.

"You need to eat more," I'd push, but again Jonathan would insist that his sensitive stomach limited his appetite. The more he starved, exhibiting complete control over his food, the more I was drawn back to bulimia, bingeing and purging more frequently. It became this warped competition, with my anger growing with each bite he refused to eat. I kept trying to bait Jonathan to eat, even explaining bluntly that a six-foot-two man needed to weigh more than one hundred sixty pounds if he wanted to be attractive.

After Jonathan squashed my domestic fantasies with his aversion to food, I gave up cooking and chose restaurants in the neighborhood that had single-stall bathrooms. Luckily, he lived in a different part of town than I used to, and no one here was familiar with my eating habits. Instead of slipping into an anorexic codependency, which I would have preferred, I reacted by recovering my bulimia with a fervor. Given the choice between anorexia and bulimia, I would always choose to starve, but when it came to eating disorders, I never had the choice. Watching him pecking at his steamed chicken and waterlogged vegetables sent me into a rage, with me competing to prove to Jonathan that, unlike him, I was not afraid to eat.

Look at me eating my seventh dinner roll, rich creamy pasta, and yes, of course I'll have dessert.

He was way too busy marveling at my speedy metabolism to notice how often I slipped off to the restroom in order to relieve my stomach of its contents. Over dinner, Jonathan would order his seventh cup of coffee for the day, the ultimate appetite suppressant, as I went for the iced tea–lemonade mix, or if it were tense I'd have that glass of wine.

"I love watching you eat," he'd marvel. "You eat like a truck driver and never gain weight. I wish I could do that."

I finally climbed out of the denial river and realized that this guy would not rescue me into a better life. In many ways, he was a bigger mess than I was. Because I had never had a man take care of me, I believed love from the right man would cure my bulimia—with a man's love I would not need to work to cure myself. So I was devastated when I realized that Jonathan was a problem, not the solution I had been seeking.

My black woman's hips, butt, and thighs were thicker than those of this skinny white man I went home to each night, and it pushed my insanity buttons. As warped as my self-perception was, I knew I could not be with a man who made me feel like a whale, and so I began to search for an exit.

I started to pull away from Jonathan, angry at myself for choosing yet another unsatisfying relationship to try to sate my insatiable hunger. I had sold my family and friends on this new love as the stable centerpiece of my future, and they all had exhaled with relief. So without saying anything to anyone, I began to plot my escape from this new horror movie that had taken over my life. I had to do it in a way that didn't cause alarm; once more, people were noticing certain things about my behavior and worrying about me.

I decided to go home to New York for an indeterminate amount of time. Since I had most of my things in storage, I only needed to pack my clothing and the assorted odds and ends I had moved into Jonathan's duplex.

"I need to go home and be with my family for a little while. I'm burned out on Hollywood," I explained to Jonathan in desperation. I did everything short of giving him the *It's not you, it's me* send-off, but I couldn't break up with him. He loved me.

"When are you coming back?" he pleaded, asking me to reconsider.

"Soon," I lied, knowing that once I was out that door I would be off again on my quest for someone to offer me the safety, love, and support I was obsessed with finding. After I left we spoke on the phone daily, then weekly, until our communication was weaned down to almost nothing. A couple of months later, frustrated with waiting for my return, Jonathan demanded a real answer.

"Are you even planning to come back?" he shouted.

No longer able to avoid the inevitable, I finally told him some version of the truth. "I don't want to be in Los Angeles anymore. I need to find myself, and I need to be here in New York to do that."

The truth was I desperately needed a man to take care of me, not the other way around. I didn't want to worry if he was eating and to get pulled into his obsessive-compulsive relationship with food; after all I had my own. I couldn't love someone who took such poor care of himself; how could I trust him to take care of me? There should be a rule: one screwed-up person to a relationship, please.

New York

While my seeds of bulimia were firmly planted in the soil of my New York childhood, they came to a full bloom in Los Angeles, where things had spiraled out of control. To my unenlightened mind, the price of returning to normal was as inexpensive—or, in my broke case, as expensive—as a one-way coach ticket back to the Big Apple. I believed that when I touched down on the East Coast, all of my problems with food would be left in the fog and fantasyland of Los Angeles. It didn't occur to me that three years earlier I had fled New York, narrowly escaping a stay in a mental institution, in search of a saner future free of heartbreak in Los Angeles. The pain of my breakup with Gary and my failed suicide attempt should have at least crossed my mind as my plane landed in New York, but they didn't.

I was unable to see the parallels with my mother's behavior, how I, like she, lacked the ability to ride out life's storms, both internal and external. Childhood taught me that a move of even four blocks away could transform the way you saw your life, at least until the next move.

I could not bear to sit through the pain. My answer to all challenges and problems came in the form of motion. Like the premise of the shooting game I grew up playing on visits to Coney Island, where the metal duck moves in quick, circular, constant motions, I felt that if I never stopped moving, I would never be a target. Just like the metal duck, I was not aware of whether the motion moved me forward or I was simply spinning in circles; the motion itself was key to preservation.

As often happens with siblings who are raised in chaotic and unpredictable circumstances, my sister Renee took the opposite route. After the end of her abusive first marriage, when she'd finally said "enough" and left him, she landed swiftly in a second, without any thought to the nightmare that came before. Her route to security was a straight one: she took a dependable state job as a corrections officer, where the outdated mantra "In by twenty, out by forty" kept her focused on the future. Of course the officers guarding the prisoners had no clue that they, too, would become handcuffed to the place, with few able to afford early retirement.

One of the prime benefits of my sister's state job was a thirty-year mortgage that required a minimum of forty years to afford. Joining the state correctional department meant beginning as low person on the totem pole, taking the worst shifts, and often being forced to work overtime. The stress of my sister's new job on her marriage proved a perfect opportunity for me. I made a deal with my sister and brother-in-law to nanny her two kids from her previous marriage and their one child together. I would live with them and watch their kids for nine months, until my sister could graduate to a more acceptable shift. I planned to use that time to focus on my writing, which had taken a backseat to my interest in food. Even though I had no real indication that I was anything but marginally talented,

I soldiered on, ever hopeful that I would achieve some success as a writer. After all, I hadn't exactly done well working in a structured environment.

So I took up residence on "the Rock," the local name for Staten Island. With Manhattan a ferry ride away, Staten Island might as well have been Rhode Island. Of the four outer boroughs, this was the least accessible and required the most work to enter and exit. It bore no resemblance to a major metropolis; if you drove far enough onto the island, you'd come to rural areas with horses and pastures. On weekdays the ferry stopped working at midnight, and if you got caught on the Manhattan side you had to travel to the end of Brooklyn and catch a bus across the Verrazano-Narrows Bridge, up to a two-hour trip one way.

I found everything about Staten Island isolating and uninteresting. For my sister—unlike her time in the Park Hill projects on the other side of the island, once home to multiple family members and where my ex-brother-in-law slung drugs and wore a groove in my sister's backside—life here was far less oppressive. Her building, a high-rise on Victory Boulevard, came with a doorman and a pool. It was only a ten-minute walk to the ferry for those times I had cabin fever and needed to flee the Rock.

Since I was on unemployment, I had limited resources for bingeing and assumed that the change in financial status would deter me from my troubles with food. Naïveté and denial are hallmarks of eating disorders. But like a homeless heroin addict who always finds the means for a fix, I had plenty of ingenuity and determination when it came to my habit. I'd travel from Staten Island to Manhattan, a trip that easily took three hours if I made the ferry, to buy my favorite bagels just so I could throw them up. I learned how to binge on a budget; a box of Bisquick and milk could mean pancakes, biscuits, and muffins for days. I'd sit my three-year-old niece in front of a movie or television show and fall face-first into a binge, swallowing enough food in under an hour to feed my sister's family (who lived on a tight budget in order to afford their high-rise apartment) for a week.

Twenty-plus years ago the terms *eating disorder, bulimia, anorexia, binge eating*, and *compulsive eater* had not yet seeped into the popular lexicon, which made it easier to stay in denial. I preferred to think of it simply as "my little problem with food." Sure I had heard the words *anorexic* and *bulimic*, but to me that meant girls like Karen Carpenter, not someone who starved for a few days and then shoved laxatives or her fingers down her throat after taking that first bite. So for the most part I remained blissfully uneducated about the depth of my food and emotional problems. I assumed it was something I could control through will power, the perfect new diet, or the right relationship. At the very least I would grow tired of my head in the toilet and dump the entire practice like some phase, easily leaving it in the past like bed-wetting.

After all, puking my guts up no longer guaranteed I'd be rail thin. My body rebelled from the constant starvation and held on to any extra calories it could. Most people who knew me at the time considered me "thin," "small," "tiny," all of the words I found comforting and validating enough to keep the bad behavior going. Rarely did I weigh more than one hundred and twenty pounds, and on a five-foot-five-inch frame, that was considered normal.

"Oh my goodness—how the hell do you eat so much and stay so thin?" people asked me all the time.

And usually they'd answer the question themselves, without any input from me, which I preferred because I had spent so much time lying about my relationship with food already.

"You are so lucky to have that metabolism," they'd say by way of explanation.

Metabolism was how people who, unknowingly, sat through binge meals with me could justify my eating twice what they did while remaining sizes smaller. Of course, I could never bring myself to reveal my diet secret, which caused tremendous shame and self-loathing already.

Each morning I promised myself a day of freedom from throwing up. After all, I'd been craving this writing time for years. But once I took that first bite, I'd be off and running, hand in hand with my little problem, consumed with food lust, oblivious to the existence of anything else. Bulimia became my most faithful lover, filling me up, and by the end of the binge I purged myself of guilt and shame and feelings of insecurity, and for those few blissful moments afterward I felt at peace. All the doubts, shame, and fear dissipated, and I was no longer unworthy or unlovable. I felt capable and in control; I believed that I could handle my life and that I would be victorious.

But those feelings never lasted. They'd soon wear off, and I would be my broken, shattered self once more. I'd grow overwhelmed and disgusted with myself, and I needed the food to comfort me, until I'd become so stuffed after bingeing that I hated myself for losing control all over again. The uncontrollable need to purge would overtake me, and the cycle would continue, beginning anew each time I took that next bite.

For a while, I was able to control my episodes, limiting them to the mornings and early afternoons, before my eleven-year-old niece and ten-year-old nephew returned home from school. But as with all addictions, the honeymoon period—the early time of maintaining any control—didn't last long. Within weeks I was using food to numb myself around the clock, and I required more, and my methods worked less and less. Instead of catering to my nieces and nephew, as I was supposed to do and as my sister counted on me to do, I catered to my addiction, riding along on that self-obsessed destructive path until the wheels almost came off.

Whenever I was able to take a break from babysitting because my sister or her husband had time off from work and could be home with the kids, I escaped to Manhattan, easily the most populated isolation tank in the world. This city is built for those with a desire to be invisible, to blend in and become part of the atmosphere in the blockbuster fashion, business, and real estate capital. I'd stay with friends, far removed in upbringing and attitude from the instability of my childhood and my Hollywood life.

I'd wander around aimlessly, walking from the ferry at Battery Park to the Upper West Side, which is at least a hundred city blocks, to stay in shape. I took everything further than a normal person would have. If a three-mile walk kept you in shape, then I would attempt a thirty-mile walk, imagining my legs growing smaller and fitter with every step. I wanted to be skinny by any means necessary, which included abusing exercise.

Like an award-winning actress, I had the uncanny ability to transform myself into whatever role a relationship required. With my fabulously urban friends, I became a show-business insider, regaling them with gossip about celebrities. Being an attractive girl with a few great connections, I had a knack for wrangling myself into the best clubs, events, and restaurants—all the while reveling in the knowledge that I could access whatever hot-spot I wanted. I'd spin on a social whirl, flitting from one venue to another, dinner parties in penthouses, movie premieres, and fun weekends in the Hamptons. But inside I had never felt so helpless, isolated, and depressed.

I spent lots of my free time in Brooklyn at Clean's house, where he lived with his wife, Margot, and new baby. For many years he rode in like the Lone Ranger, quick to rescue me from myself and things like late rent and parking tickets when I lived in Los Angeles. Clean maintained a bicoastal life, so he remained one of the few people I had a consistent relationship with during my "out of control with food" phase in L.A. When my bulimia got out of hand and I could no longer afford to feed my hunger, I'd land on the doorstep of Clean's house, where magically I had not worn out my welcome. He loved me like a little sister and cosigned for loads of irresponsible behavior, always willing to listen to the revolving adventures that substituted for a stable love life. He knew my daddy thing and how it made it improbable that I'd ever trust a man to love me. He'd chastise me that all I needed was to stop having such strong opinions and learn to listen to—in other words "obey"—a man.

But despite his chauvinism, I trusted Clean. I'd always been there for him, and then Margot, and I only hoped they failed to notice I'd become far more of a taker, behavior that began with my secret disorder and that was getting worse.

Clean and Margot kept lots of cash laying around their house and stuffed into jackets they had taken off and tossed in the closet. Somewhere in their home, I could always find the spare twenty to feed my fix. Had I asked Clean for the money, he would have simply handed it to me, but I did not want to answer any questions as to why money slipped through my fingers. Like an addict who had hit a soft bottom, I didn't question the depths and distance I traveled to feed my disease. Nothing and no one was more important than my bulimic behavior. I didn't think Clean noticed the missing bills I had slid out of his pockets or picked up from dresser tops, but I always had an excuse at the ready or a strong declaration of innocence, just in case it was ever needed.

My sister Renee had always lived on a tight budget, and I knew that my eating her out of house and home had placed a strain on her relationship, so I'd try to replace the binge food whenever I could in order to cover my tracks. I spent so much time puking my guts out in the lone bathroom of my sister's apartment that I often worried that my nieces or nephew would hear me. There had been so many close calls, with them begging to use the bathroom as I ran water to hide the sounds of throwing up. I'd clean the puke from the floor and empty the toilet before washing my face and swinging the door open, wearing an expression of pure innocence.

It felt like a circus juggling routine, keeping my charges busy while I binged and then purged, cleaned up, hid the evidence, helped with homework—all the while pretending to be focused on something other than the next binge.

When it was just me and my three-year-old niece at home, I had a simpler solution. I bought my favorite kids' movie, *Willie Wonka and the Chocolate Factory*. I'd put it on, place her in front of the TV, and slip into the bathroom to throw up.

Renee and I were so tight that I had to work extra hard to keep my secret hidden from her. I had made a pact with myself never to binge when Renee was home, which was impossible. I'd be forced to have one slow binge so as not to arouse suspicion, then I'd try to time to my shower so that I would have an excuse for being in the bathroom so long. Of course, this didn't always work, and a few times I was forced to keep down the food. And there were times when I took too long in the bathroom and almost got caught. She once came close to busting me, but I lied and said I threw up because I had food poisoning.

I had just spent the weekend in an alternate universe: at a penthouse on the Upper East Side with a wraparound deck that overlooked the river. I even managed a binge-free trip to Dean and DeLuca, expensive champagne, and intimate conversation without throwing up for two days, so I felt cured. At that moment, I saw bingeing and purging as distant relatives too far removed to reach out and affect me again. But I couldn't have been more wrong.

"Stephanie, we need to talk." Renee caught me at the door, her tone deflating my temporary euphoria at being able to control "my little food problem."

I followed her onto the balcony, my mind racing at all the offenses she could be confronting me with—running up her phone bills, ignoring her children, lying about food— but throwing up wasn't even on my list. My confidence came from the knowledge that I had been very careful when she was around.

"Sy told me that you've been throwing up."

And there it was, my biggest fear: her older daughter had figured out what I was up to in the bathroom. "I have a sensitive stomach. It's happened a few times." I tried to sound casual even as my heart thumped so loudly I was sure she'd hear it.

"No, Stephanie. She says you do it all the time. Every day."

"Well . . . it's nothing," I lied.

"How can it be nothing?" The sound of my sister's voice crumbled me. "It's serious enough that you can't stop doing it."

The worry etched on her face made me feel horrible, which was another problem, since I spent most of my time avoiding all feelings. I did not want her to be affected by this. It was one thing for me to deal with my problems with food, but it was another to pile them on my sister, who already had three kids and a husband. Especially when I thought I could regain control and handle it. It had been so long since I had allowed anyone in my family close enough access to voice concern for me, and I didn't like it one bit. But it wasn't even worry that bothered me the most; it was the blinding light it put on my problem. I still hadn't admitted the depth of my issues to myself, so I absolutely wasn't ready for this to go through the Covington grapevine.

"You don't understand . . ." The waterworks started. "I just throw up because it helps me to deal with what Uncle John did to me." If Renee had been a cat, she would have been up on her haunches ready to attack him.

"What?" her voice shook.

"He tried to enter me when I was twelve." And the tears I had been pushing out began falling on their own. Renee wrapped her arms around me, letting her sweater soak up my tears. After I stopped crying, I took her through the events of that night.

"That motherfucker! I could kill him," she raged. "Why didn't you tell me?"

Hours later, I lay next to my sister talking late into the night. In the end, I promised to stop throwing up and to stop shutting her out of my problems. One thing I have always been secure about is my sister's love for me; she loves me purely, and we are close in a sacred, shared-childhood way, forever bonded by the rocky landscape of our upbringing. Renee loved that I had escaped our limitations and struck out on my own in search of a world far from the one of our youth. To my sister, I had become as exotic and foreign as California—beautiful, sunny, and expansive. The two of us were as familiar and different as the Atlantic and Pacific oceans, but our shared history made it impossible for us ever to become disconnected.

But even though I felt relief at having disclosed this painful event, it was not the explanation for my throwing up. I knew that and knew I was still deflecting my issues. I told my sister about the rape because it would distract her from my problems with food. I was not ready to stop bingeing and purging, and I would have done or said anything, even reveal a secret I had kept hidden from her for almost ten years. To my sister, the rape was massively larger than whatever I did with my food. That was what I needed her to think. Hell, that's what I needed to think.

Secrets didn't survive in our family, and my new revelation was no exception. I could not fault Renee for the leak, because I'm positive she went looking for support from someone who knew the perpetrator. To understand my sister is to know that she is the least confrontational person you'd ever meet—that is, until you push her too far. Then she can battle with the best of us.

But as soon as one person in the Covington family knew something, it spread like a virus, shooting through the veins in my large extended family. Time had not mellowed my rage at my uncle's molestation of me, and I no longer cared if someone knew. In fact, I probably wanted my family to know. Over the years I witnessed my uncle at family gatherings lapping up the praise from my female relatives, and I wanted to wipe that smirk of self-satisfaction off his face. What he had done to me had paralyzed my ability to trust and to let myself be loved.

Aunts, cousins, and even my grandmother weighed in, most refusing to believe my uncle could have done such a horrible thing. Even after his ouster from the New York Stock Exchange for insider trading, my family still considered him some kind of hero. When they bought his story of being fired from Wall Street because he was so magnanimous that he took the fall for other stockbrokers who had more to lose, I should have known he would never be viewed as guilty of anything in their eyes.

And my confession affected my sister to such a degree that it overshadowed my food problem, which, in view of the sexual abuse, she decided didn't warrant being retold to any relatives— which was exactly what I hoped would happen. I had been in California too long, the land of make believe, where the sun had fried my brain, and my already overactive imagination had shifted into overdrive.

But like everything unpleasant in our long and complicated history, my family shoved the story of my uncle's abuse into the closet, pretending it didn't exist. I needed to remember that we were family, and family sticks together through thick, thin, and child molestation.

Sitting at the Thanksgiving dinner table across from my uncle that year made me feel dirty, as if I were being molested again. It was not like in the earlier years, when no one knew my story. By now, news had reached everyone old enough to be seated around that adult table. Whether they said something or not, I could tell by the nervous eyes darting between my uncle and me that they had heard the story. So this Thanksgiving, my family members were all coconspirators, and as they shoveled in humongous helpings of the holiday feast, I extended my rage to include them.

Renee hovered over me like a mother bear, but it didn't lessen the pain. And no matter how loud their boisterous laughter, it could not drown out my sense that I had nothing to be thankful for. All these years later, it still had not occurred to my relatives to protect me or to make him pay for his crimes.

I tried to pretend that my uncle didn't exist. He shot me smug, dirty looks across the table, as if I were the one who had molested him, not the other way around. So as my family moved on to the usual postdinner card games, loudly arguing strategies, I separated myself from their happy banter, shoveling food down my throat to eradicate the rage I felt bubbling up inside. To calm the inner child, once again wounded by their inability to rescue me from the monster in the family, I binged at the table and then purged in the bathroom, hoping the pipes didn't get clogged by the steady swell of vomit. But it didn't really matter. If they didn't care about me, then I didn't care much about them either, or about myself.

"Can you do me a favor and wait for the cable guy?" Renee had asked me a few days after Thanksgiving, just before she and her family mysteriously disappeared for the day.

Shortly after, my mother arrived, unannounced but on time. I had been tricked by my sister, who knew I would not have agreed to be a sitting duck awaiting my mother's arrival.

My mother generally avoided large family gatherings where she could witness the siblings she had strung together sharing an intimacy that made her feel excluded, so she had not been at our Thanksgiving dinner. She would always be more the mother than the older sister to her younger siblings, and none of them needed a mother anymore. I assumed she made the special trip to discuss my childhood tragedy.

"Stephanie." She reached to embrace me, and without prompting my body froze up, stiffening against her touch. I loved my mother, but her physical affection felt alien and off-putting. I could never reconcile her touch being offered so easily when I had craved it so throughout my childhood, and each time it happened the cells in my body went into a state of shock.

"Mom." I pulled away, hoping she wouldn't notice or take it personally. I wasn't what you would call a hugger.

"Why didn't you tell me?" Her voice broke, revealing that she was not as strong as she pretended to be. Her very presence at my sister's was a sign of how this news had shaken her world.

"I couldn't tell you." I started pacing, unable to stay still. My body, which rarely sweated, began to overheat. I wanted to get away from myself, my mother, and the conversation I knew was now unavoidable.

"But why?" The question came out as a plea.

I dropped into a chair at the dining room table and faced her. She slumped down in the chair next to me.

"I didn't want you to kill him."

"You're right." She spat out the words with enough venom to maim her younger brother: "I would have killed that motherfucker!"

"I couldn't let you go to jail—" But she cut me off before I could finish my thought: *I couldn't let you go to jail and every-*

*one would hate me and my shaky foundation would collapse and
I'd be passed around to relatives who had less interest in me and
I would be alone. I couldn't tell you because I needed my mother
and I didn't want to be alone.*

She was shouting. "You are *my child*. It is *my job* to protect
you from perverts like my brother. I should have done that. *You
should have never gone through any of this!*"

"I'm OK. I went to a therapist, and I'm fine now." I lied,
desperate for this conversation to end. I wanted this to be a sitcom moment, wrapped up painlessly in under thirty minutes.

Though it was not over quickly, I was able to calm down
my mother between her chain-smoking drags on her king size
Kools. I did not lie about my reasons for not telling her, though
I did underplay the effect the molestation had on my life, especially how I was unable now to handle real intimacy and why
I never felt worthy of success or a normal life. It hurt me to
see my mother in so much pain, and I said whatever I could
to take away the sting of her finding out what my uncle had
done to me.

Even as an adult, I did not feel quite comfortable being
alone with my mother, and certainly not talking about anything personal. It was one thing to receive her flurry of letters,
extolling her great faith in my career, her love for me, and her
regret that she had not given me a better childhood. But sitting face-to-face with her, I had the image of a prisoner seeing
a long-lost parent across the Plexiglas window in a maximum-
security visiting area. I loved my mother, but we were both better at expressing our closeness over the telephone or in a letter. I
felt exposed and vulnerable, craving a binge, a way to transport
myself away from a conversation I never wanted to have.

"I asked him, and he denied it, but I want you to know that
I believe you. I always would have believed you," she said.

Just as I'd been at the time of the abuse, I was certain now
that my mother and Renee would have taken my side without question. But I was equally sure the revelation would have
destroyed the makeshift family my mother had worked so hard

to pull together. She'd spent so much of our childhood worrying about someone taking advantage of her three daughters, to the point of paranoia, and here she had trusted the man who had violated our innocence.

I needed to comfort her, to take the focus off me. As my mother continued to question me and blame herself, each answer unraveling the very fabric of her existence, I began to paint a story of courage and triumph and bravery. I needed to deflect her pain, which had magnified in the mirror of her daughter's shattered childhood. I was my mother's baby, the youngest and the most familiar. We had had intense moments of closeness, and although they were rare, they were possible only between us. Long into the evening we talked, and I struggled to repair the damage to my mother's soul. I just wanted her to be fine, and I wanted to retreat into my disease without an audience checking to see if I was suicidal.

Hours later, my sister came home, looking guilty for having cornered me like this. But I couldn't be mad at my sister. I understood that all she wanted was for me to be OK. I thought back to when my cousin had told me about my mother's almost abortion. I now understood that she had innocently believed this information would confirm my mother's love for me rather than validating my belief that I was a huge burden to my mother.

I decided then and there, after my mother's visit, that my family had become too close for comfort. I needed my secret relationship with food to stay a secret, and so once again I began to plot my escape.

Location,
Location, Location

"You can carry all that?" Renee stood at the curb as I wrestled with a pile of things I needed to get me through the next little while. I was headed for a temporary stay in Vermont.

"I carried Courtney around for the last year. This is nothing!"

"Don't talk about my baby." She painted on a fake scowl, but she wasn't good at hiding her concern. Three children, two troubled sisters, and a mother bound to change her entire life at any moment turned up the volume on Renee's maternal instinct, toward me as well as her own kids.

"I'm used to moving," I joked, hoping to relax the tension in her face and to avoid another heart to heart.

"That don't mean you have to keep doing it."

"I'll be back. Besides, how many little sisters do you have?"

I had promised my sister, over flowing tears and tea, that I would stop throwing up, sobbing revelations that I knew my behavior was not healthy. In other words, I told my sister whatever she needed to hear in order to stave off her concern.

I did not want to worry about anyone watching my eating, monitoring how long I stayed in the bathroom, or looking to see if my face had puffed out at the cheeks or if there were broken blood vessels under my watery eyes. I did not want to stop throwing up. I needed my bulimia in order to survive, and no one and nothing could convince me to give up what had become my sole coping skill. I knew all about the physical, medical, and emotional consequences that might occur if I continued to throw up, but I could not stop, and no one was going to make me. It didn't matter to me that death was on the top of the list of possible consequences.

I had slipped further underground, hiding my disease with a calculated precision. *How much time do I have before people come home? How many eggs were in the fridge when Renee left?* I learned to replace everything exactly the way she had left it in the kitchen, down to cutting the butter at exactly the same spot. It took Herculean efforts not to be discovered, especially if someone came home in the midst of a binge, and I'd be forced to sit with food in my stomach. So I learned how to throw up into garbage bags. My relationship with myself and food was so warped I did not see stopping as an option. Rather than working to overcome my addiction, I put all my energy into plotting how to escape prying eyes and questions.

Relief had come in the form of acceptance into a writers' colony in Vermont. A few writer friends had suggested I apply in order to jump-start my creativity, telling me I would be fueled by living in a creative environment. I knew nothing about Vermont except that it was far from New York, which had become the new center of my disease.

The only problem had been money—or rather lack of money. My unemployment insurance was fast approaching closure, so I needed to figure out how to get my hands on a quick influx of cash. I did the math and concluded that I could survive for a month to six weeks in Vermont if I had an extra three hundred dollars.

A lightbulb went on: I would ask my emotionally and physically unavailable father. He'd definitely come through this time. The perfect solution!

In retrospect, I can only chalk up my enthusiasm for the idea to denial and insanity. One time I had borrowed rent money from my father, and he made the loan under the threat of completely cutting off contact with me unless I repaid him in full on the agreed-upon date, which was my next payday. I had exactly two weeks to repay him, or he would disappear from my life. I had never before or since paid off a debt in such a timely manner.

But I had already decided that Vermont was the remedy necessary to end my food addiction. Surely I wouldn't be tempted by the scent of bagels and doughnuts in Vermont. I would be seduced by the open air, creative writers, and a lack of distraction for anything but my craft.

My father had often been described as not having a generous bone in his body, and he made no apologies about his inability to part with his hard-earned money. But feeling vulnerable and desperate, I decided to reach out to a man who had always held his money (love) at a distance too high for me to reach. I still did not have his home number, so I had no choice but to wait until morning and call him at his office. I guess I still held out the hope that this time he wouldn't let me down, that he would morph into the father of my childhood fantasies, the father starring in those tales I told in the elementary school yard that had him rescuing hostages and taking out bad guys. I needed him to come to my rescue; I needed to make another attempt to see if he loved me.

My calls were still being met with suspicion, just as they had been ever since I had first gotten his phone number at twelve years old. He always assumed that if I called him, surely I wanted something, and to him that meant money. He could never believe I would reach out for attention, kindness, love, or just to see how he was doing. In ten years I had probably called him an average of once a month. I remember asking for half a dozen things in that time, two of which he had given me: a hundred dollars for my cheerleading uniform and the loan for my rent. So I never understood why he still tripped so hard on my telephone calls.

Of course, today I felt more than a little guilty. Usually I would be smug and volunteer up front that I was simply calling to say hello or to talk. But I did have a motive, and I had to make it clear.

"Hey, Dad." I tried to sound upbeat and cheerful.

"What, Stephanie—I'm working." He sounded slightly annoyed. It felt as if he'd connected to a psychic who informed him that his daughter would be calling to hit him up for funds, and he wanted to cut me off at the outset.

"Dad, I got accepted to a writers' colony in Vermont!" I bubbled.

"How are you going to afford that?" He went straight to the point.

"It's free," I lied, refusing to acknowledge the small weekly fee, since I had already worked that into my budget.

"So you're just going to go to someplace with a bunch of writers and do what?" He wanted a plan. My father was an accountant, so everything had to balance out on a spreadsheet and still make sense. He didn't understand anything unless it involved absolutes.

"Dad, it's an opportunity for me to write. It's my dream." How he could fail to comprehend the magnitude of this opportunity? To my father, dreams were something you put on hold until life swept past you, and they grew into unfulfilled desires.

"Well, it sounds crazy to me."

I paused, then said, "I have almost everything I need. I'm just a little short."

"You want money from me for this?" I imagined his dark face burning with righteous anger.

"Dad, I have everything except two hundred dollars." I lowered my cushier figure of three hundred on the spot, prompted by his attitude. It was clear that if I managed to talk my father out of two hundred dollars, I should take the money and run right to Vermont and never look back.

"I don't have that kind of money," he shouted.

This would have made sense if I had gone to my mother, who had never earned more than twenty thousand dollars a year in her entire life. My father, on the other hand, was a senior executive, having toiled for twenty years in the accounting department at IBM. Although I couldn't count his money, my father was single and didn't own a home or have any of the hefty expenses of the upwardly mobile, except his hobby of tennis. That, coupled with all the money he saved by not writing child support checks to my mother, meant he had to have two hundred dollars. I could have backed down and accepted his answer, but I knew he was lying, and now I was mad.

"Dad, I have hardly ever asked you for anything in my entire life. I need this," I pleaded, trying to pull at his heart strings, if he had any.

"I'll have to ask a friend for the money and call you back." He offered some hope before hanging up the phone without signing off.

I waited by the phone for my father's call, imagining countless scenarios, until the next day when the call finally came.

"I asked a friend, who said if any of his four daughters asked him for money to go gallivanting off to some writers' colony, he'd tell her to get a job."

I had his answer. With my father, arguing or trying to make him feel guilty made no sense. Once he had made a decision, he was satisfied and secure, and he stuck to it. He did not care what I or anyone else thought about his behavior, and he would be able to sleep soundly at night. According to my father, the world we live in does not subsist on socialism; we are a country of social, material, and political capitalism. His motto was "Every man for himself." But since he had failed to support me growing up, I thought of it as "Every man, woman, and child for himself and herself." I joked that if money were needed to be rescued from the *Titanic* and I reached my hand toward my father, I would have surely gone down with the ship. He would have felt no remorse for saving only himself.

Nonetheless, I arrived by bus in Dorset, Vermont, three hundred dollars shy of my goal. But I had made a life out of transcending my financial limitations, and I decided that this experience would be no different. I also decided to stop throwing up and to reform myself amid the serene beauty of New England. This seemed like an easy feat, since it would probably be difficult to locate the supermarket-chain bargain foods I had come to depend on for my binges.

But unfortunately for me, located in the idyllic town of Dorset was the delectable Peltier's, a charming country store known especially for its baked goods. As soon as you entered, the smell of fresh-baked croissants, muffins, and breads, along with the kind owners, greeted you and made you feel blessed to be born and to be standing in this exact space. In other words, you were one lucky person to have landed in such a perfect spot in the universe.

But to me it was pure hell. It didn't matter if you had an eating disorder, the scents wafting out of Peltier's could trigger an immediate craving, making you walk in that direction whether you meant to or not in order to get your fix. Each day I would awake with a promise: *I will not go to Peltier's.* But to support my habit I'd somehow manipulate the money from somewhere, often landing at the front door as the store was closing for the day. If food were in fact love, then we'd all want to live in the warm bosom of Peltier's store.

I quickly wound up making friends with two other residents—Stephen, who was the colony superstar, having written parts of his bestselling novel there, and Sebastian, whose quick wit staved off hours of boredom. The three of us sought out ways to avoid the other residents, most of whom possessed one quirk too many. We'd put ourselves on the same writing schedules and meet for breaks, hiding out in one another's rooms. We also started cooking together, making healthy dinners. There would be days when the high of writing and having this makeshift family made me forget to obsess about food. Magically, I believed I was cured and that it would be easy to stop my disordered eating and abandon bulimia for the next stage of my life, where sanity would no longer be a goal but a reality. I believed that I could finally control my relationship with food.

This fantasy existence was fine for the first weeks, until I began to run out of money. Then I panicked and had to get creative. At the time I had no clue that situations reminiscent of my childhood poverty were a huge trigger for my bulimia. At a subconscious level, financial vulnerability meant possible starvation; reversion to that powerlessness of childhood threatened to send me into a raging bout of bulimia.

Strapped for cash, I convinced the guys of the benefits of arranging communal dinners with the other colony residents. I explained that it would make our self-imposed exile from desirable urban locations more palatable. I created the menu, doled out cooking assignments, collected the money, and shopped. And though the majority of the money went to the dinners, I siphoned off enough to feed my addiction between communal dinners. I needed that influx of cash to keep my true love, bulimia, alive. I didn't spend too much time questioning the morality of my behavior. The goal of obtaining binge food dwarfed any other reality.

Sebastian, Steve, and I developed a love of garage sales and auctions, which were listed in a local penny-saver circular. When we bumped up against writer's block and couldn't find our way out, we'd hitchhike to auctions in nearby communities. Each weekend we'd explore a little farther, going to auctions in

New Hampshire and Rhode Island, where we'd marvel at the antiques and paintings that Sebastian was always convinced were stolen masterpieces worth a fortune.

The one auction that stood apart from the rest required Sebastian and me to hitchhike miles outside of Dorset to a remote country location. In Manchester or Dorset, it is easy to forget that parts of Vermont are very rural. We arrived at what appeared to be an abandoned airstrip in the middle of nowhere. Here I came, swinging my long extension braids, clunking my black cowboy boots, dressed in a black leather jacket. I was the quintessential urban girl. Entering this old hangar, I nudged Sebastian, both of us aware it was too late to turn and run without causing a commotion. Off to one side was a makeshift table where women in *Little House on the Prairie* dresses sold cakes, pies, cookies, and sodas. I couldn't pass up the chance to purchase cheap binge food for later. The woman behind the counter stared in awe at my exotic look as I decided which treats were most bingeworthy. I was too busy looking around to notice that all movement and noise had stopped as every head turned in my direction.

"Is this the auction?" I asked one of the women hawking baked goods.

"Up on the stage." She pointed to a raised platform straight down the end of the aisle. "Everything is sold by the box. You can go take a look in the boxes."

I marched up to the front and climbed the steps onto the stage, only to find boxes filled with plastic cups, jelly jars, and other assorted items you'd dig out of the dumpster in even the lowest-income urban neighborhood. I turned to see Sebastian coming up the aisle.

"This is crap," he whispered, holding up a jelly jar, speaking in his prissiest queen voice, which made me howl with laughter. "Let's get out of here."

He hustled me down the aisle and out the door, and eventually we found a hot young local to drive us back to Dorset. Once in the car Sebastian couldn't wait to check the racial temperature of the neighbors. The delight in his voice was palpable.

"Stephanie, it was like people were seeing a purple giraffe when you walked in there. You should have seen their faces." He turned to our driver. "Do you have any blacks around here?" he asked.

"No, most folks never seen a black person close up. And you look like one of those Rastafarians."

I could tell by his smile that he thought he was complimenting me, so I didn't bother to lay into him.

When it came time to leave Vermont, it was because my money had run out, and all the charm in the world wasn't enough to convince the owner of the colony to give me a free pass to stay. My only option was returning to my sister's house in Staten Island, which didn't feel like much of an option at all. The great thing about Vermont is that it allowed me to keep my real life (read: problems) at bay, even tricking me into believing I was cured, since I had stopped throwing up all day every day. I had even managed to cultivate a couple of bulimia-free days. I didn't know how I would be able to continue to be semi-healthy in New York, where the stress of life felt insurmountable. I believed I could not survive without my main coping mechanism.

Luckily, or so I thought, my ticket out arrived in the form of a musician ex-boyfriend reappearing in my life. Dee asked me to visit him in London, an offer I promptly accepted. Not the type to meet me at the airport with flowers and kindness, he gave me directions to his place.

Within one hour of entering my rocker boyfriend's home, I happily swallowed my first pill of the drug ecstasy, unaware that he preferred to live his life in a permanently altered state. It took three days for my appetite to return, and those three days were bliss. Not only did I stop bingeing and purging, but I had lost all interest in food. Dee and I talked late into the night about our deep and lasting love, and we even began to plan our fairy-tale future. I finally felt I had attained what eluded me my entire life: a man who loved me.

In those three heady, drugged-out days, I vowed to stop throwing up in order to be healthy for my future with Dee. I pictured life as a musician's wife, traveling from Sweden to Australia to Argentina only to return home to repack for another adventure. Who would have time to think about bulimia with that kind of life? My desperation to believe in our happily-ever-after overshadowed the reality that three days of togetherness were not enough time to make real-life decisions or to even know each other. We had never actually spent more than a few days together, and yet here I wanted to tattoo myself to him for life. I had become Alice sinking down the rabbit hole, begging someone—anyone—to pull me back up into reality.

As a novice user, I also did not understand that Dee's words were spoken through a drug haze and that his promises of coupled bliss would last only as long as the high. When the drugs wore off, it was clear that the expiration date on our romance had also passed. After three days of starvation and the realization that I had traveled thousands of miles simply to get laid, not to have my need for long-term love fulfilled, I fell into a deep depression.

Dee could not deal with my neediness and my constant questions about our relationship. He insisted on a looser, more carefree, rock-and-roll relationship, in which the woman took what was offered and demanded little in return. To him, my expectations of the life he'd sweetly promised over the telephone and in our drug-induced talks were too stifling. He needed his freedom.

"Stephanie, I don't know where I am going from one week to the next. I could be in Japan or Madagascar, and it wouldn't be fair to keep you waiting," he finally said.

I knew a kiss-off when I heard one. I could not sit with the discomfort that I would have to return to America and the remains of my already wrecked life. I had wanted London and Dee to be my escape hatch, and once again my expectations had come crashing back to reality. I still had a week left before my flight home when things reached a breaking point.

Stuck where I clearly wasn't wanted, when Dee went off to the studio I took the little money I did have and began bingeing and purging all over London. I fell headfirst back into the food, swallowing down disappointment and shame with each bite. I craved the numb, calming feeling I got after vomiting.

When my money ran out, I didn't let the fact that I was tone deaf stop me from singing in the Tube for money. I warbled my way through eighties R&B songs for tips. I learned how to avoid arrests by sticking close to the regulars, emboldened by the need to buy food to support my habit. I would have done almost anything to be able to continue practicing bulimia. It was the only thing that stood between me and a successful suicide attempt.

Once again, I promised myself that I would no longer seek out a man to save me. I vowed to stop believing that if I had a man who loved me, I would not need anything else, that the love of a man meant I did not need to love myself. A man could not love me into sanity.

Before long, I landed back in Los Angeles, crashing at Kelly's place, convinced that this was where I could finally stop throwing up. In less than thirty minutes, I could hike in the mountains or drive to the ocean and meditate overlooking the Pacific. How could I expect to be abstinent in a crowded, dirty metropolis like New York or London in the first place? Yeah, Los Angeles, the birthplace of my bulimia, would be where I'd find my cure. I was convinced.

Dating for Doughnuts

Wearing out both the patience and the economic welcome mat of all my friends, I now needed a way to afford to feed my insatiable hunger. I waited tables on the weekends and worked in an office at a nine-to-five, but that money was not enough to support my addiction, my car insurance, and a roof over my head. So at the height of my bulimic insanity, I decided to take on a new job: dating.

The idea of making idle chitchat while some leering man attempted to coerce me into sex had always been my idea of a nightmare, the lifestyle of the single and desperate. In my world, I would meet some man I liked, we'd connect over witty conversation and a similar level of attractiveness, have wild, passionate sex, and before morning we'd be in a committed relationship, thereby skipping that uncomfortable getting-to-know-you phase.

But that was my prebulimic life, when I could afford not to date and I took pride in my independence from men. I was famous for taking breaks from men, which horrified my single girlfriends. One of the bonuses of being raised by a feminist mother in a houseful of women was having the mantra *You don't need men* drilled into my head along with a lack of focus on physical attributes. That might have been effective for girls who felt loved and nurtured. But to three girls starved of physical and emotional comfort, my mother's preaching that looks and beauty had no value fell on deaf ears. Unlike her, we were happy to live in the real world, where looks and popularity were valuable currency. They were also the one currency that was available to us. Our mother was beautiful, and no matter how she attempted to morph into average—cutting off her hair, refusing to wear makeup or flattering clothes—people continued to comment on her looks. She had the kind of fierce beauty that could not be disguised, no matter how hard she tried. And no matter how much she lectured us on the evils of self-involvement and shallow pursuits, we wanted to be beautiful, thinking beauty would make a man love us enough to make up for our absent fathers.

So I had finally arrived at a place in my life where I figured my looks and sparkling conversation could be bartered for a free meal. I had used friendship, work, compassion, humor, and family to feed my addiction up to this point, which meant I had singed most of the hands that fed me. It got me to thinking about how many times I had seen some great beauty—and I am not referring to myself that way—on the arms of some moderately attractive, chubby checkbook.

Men of unlimited means had been asking me out since I was old enough to date, but, always the romantic, I had chosen love or attraction or soulful connection over money. Years later a therapist would explain that although I thought I wanted a man to take care of me, my childhood made it impossible to trust any man that much, so I chose men who were financially incapable of carrying the burden of two of us. In other words, I had no faith in men with money. I needed to take care of myself by myself in order to feel secure and to protect myself from having the rug pulled out from under me.

My heart had a CLOSED FOR REPAIRS UNTIL FURTHER NOTICE sign nailing it shut, and the last thing I wanted when it came to men was a ray of hope. The naive belief that each time I met a new man that he would be different, more available, more honest, more open, more into me, more able to erase my painful past—that he would be a virtual magician—had died. This new idea of dating for doughnuts—or sushi or steak—allowed me to get fed while keeping control of my heart, something I had never been able to do before. In the past, as I got closer to a man, I could usually find something lovable about him, but this time I promised myself it would be different. This time I wasn't looking for some man to love me. This time I wanted one thing: food.

Had I been in a less desperate place, I would have considered this new occupation a further indication of my growing insanity. But I wasn't close to being self-aware. There were numerous examples in my life to dissuade me from this kind of dating, including my sister Cecilia, whose crack-cocaine addiction didn't start out with her begging to give ten-dollar blow jobs in a back alley to any takers. She had lived rent-free with her boyfriend, who introduced her to the drug, never intending to slip into depravity, just as I couldn't see this dating thing leading me to a worse place.

And just like my sister, unable to step back and evaluate my situation, I couldn't see any correlation between the path I was on and the one that had led to my sister's downfall. I figured it would be a simple "I'm cute/he's rich" exchange of currency.

One of the first changes that occurred from dating rich men for meals is that my palate became more sophisticated. If I was going to date for food, shouldn't I aim for better food than I could afford myself? I found myself going to the hippest four-star restaurants, developing a taste for foie gras and pasta with black truffle oil. Who wanted a Hostess chocolate cupcake when she could have a chocolate soufflé with Grand Marnier sauce?

I hadn't counted on this elevation in the quality of food, which meant I had to date more often in order to satisfy my new taste buds. Often the cost of one dinner wound up equaling half my rent. Sometimes I juggled two dates at one restaurant back to back, with a stunned waiter watching me shovel down two large meals plus extra bread and two desserts. In the words of my grandmother, I had lost my natural-born mind. Rather than seeing this as a sign of slipping further into my disease, I saw it as a positive, since my taste in food was improving. I fooled myself into believing I was moving up the socioeconomic ladder, enjoying champagne while living on a generic-beer budget.

I jokingly referred to myself as a food whore. Like a prostitute, I went on dates in exchange for payment—but it was conversation for food, not sex for money. One thing that came with bulimia was a self-loathing so extreme I could not bear the thought of being naked. To most men, the pleasure of my company was more than enough payment for a meal. If I ever got pushed or was made to feel that I had somehow promised sex for food, I had twenty-something years of feminist rhetoric to spew across the table: "How dare you think that buying me dinner meant I was obligated to sleep with you? What kind of person are you, and why would you believe women are so cheap and valueless? You need to check yourself."

I had more than my share of flowers and apologies, but after a few dates (meals), my good-girl routine grew stale, and I had to add more names to my Rolodex to keep getting fed. Like a low-income cocaine addict who could only afford the second-class drug crack, enough food for my disease—particularly good food—was out of my limited financial reach.

Instead of my former standard "No, thank you" when I was asked out by a man I had no interest in, I learned to smile as I began to evaluate the potential dining experience. Sizing up my candidate, I could equate an expensive haircut to a four-star restaurant; busted tennis shoes meant gourmet pizza and ice cream. Occasionally the busted sneakers surprised me by paying platinum all the way to five-course dinners.

Another bonus to living in Los Angeles was the wealth of gold diggers ready to share the tricks of their trade. At the gym there'd always be cute girls who managed to wear the flyest gear and weren't required to wait tables. They never understood why I didn't push for the fancy pocketbook and shopping spree.

One girl could not hide her disgust. "Girl, you could have gotten him to pay your rent. Dinner? You are stupid."

But my feminist mother would have disowned me if I played the game to that extreme, and so I settled for fine dining in restaurants with individual bathroom stalls where I could get rid of the food in privacy between courses.

A friend who knew I dated across the color line set me up on a blind date with a nice white guy from New York. I arranged to meet him at a brunch spot one block from my apartment so that I could converse, binge, and get home and purge before the butter had a chance to stick to my thighs. He was attractive enough, although the hip-hop gear, baggy jeans, gold chains, and oversized T-shirt were not my thing. I just couldn't get interested in thirty-year-olds dressing like minors. I had no idea that one day I'd become a forty-year-old rocking a mini and be proud of this accomplishment.

As the meal progressed, even the food could not hide this guy's desperation to merge with all things black.

"I'm in town for the *Soul Train* awards," he bragged.

"I don't watch those," I said. "I like the Oscars."

"My favorite writer is Connie Briscoe Hooks," he exclaimed to let me know that he had taken the time to investigate how black women really are.

"Really? I've never read her. I love Elie Wiesel's book *Reminiscences*. You should read it."

"I've never read him—is he some underground poet?"

"No, he's a Holocaust survivor, and his writing changed my life." This was true, but at this point I could have lied about being a Reagan supporter, I was so disgusted.

I couldn't help myself. The blacker he became, the whiter I became. I shoveled down my food with a growing rage. I had no choice but to listen to him because, like my mother had always told us, "Nothing in life is free, so don't ever expect no free lunch."

Of course, I was far beyond the point of common sense or heeding the advice of my elders. I had slipped full-on into insanity, becoming completely aware that the solutions I sought could not be found in men or food or exercise, and yet here I was. I remembered thinking, after I purged that meal, *There has got to be a better way.*

Resistance Is Futile

Of course it made sense that my big mouth landed me in trouble. Always the class clown, I loved regaling friends with tales of my dating escapades that I thought were funny but that they saw as troubling. What was so wrong with going out for three-hundred-dollar sushi dinners when my lights were about to get cut off? Was it my fault that not everybody got the joke?

I arrived at my friend Tracey's house where I had been summoned "to talk." Having sunk so far into my disease, I believed that my sham of being a healthy, happy, struggling artist had convinced my friends that I was doing well. I assumed that she was the one who needed to talk about some of the issues affecting her: career, home ownership, marriage, the weighty decision of whether to have children.

I would soon learn that Tracey, a friend for the past six years, had bumped into another friend of mine. Conversation began, and the shit had hit the fan. I had recently conned both of them into loaning me money . . . again. Never expecting them to see each other, I had used two separate, exaggerated excuses.

Well, when these two different Stephanie stories emerged, and the facts were not adding up, they consulted other close friends of mine, and before I knew it, a whole posse of girlfriends had weighed in on me. One thing I had learned to do since the onset of my bulimia was to keep all my friendships separate. I never would host or attend any event where I'd be forced to put two or more of my girlfriends together. Occasionally, we'd all run into one another at an audition or a party, but merging friendships was to be avoided at all costs. It was too risky. I had my old friends, friends who were like family, gym friends, acting friends, neighborhood friends, younger friends who came to me for advice, and my coffeehouse friends whom I met when I was writing, but rarely did any of these worlds intersect. Any addict who plans on continuing her addiction must keep friends isolated and a secret from one another; I meant to keep it that way.

So I was shocked to find several of my closest friends gathered together at Tracey's place. The moment I entered the room, all four of my sister-girlfriends stopped talking. Clearly, I had been the topic of their conversation. I immediately felt defensive and suspicious. After the initial surface chitchat, they closed in.

"Stephanie, we're worried about you."

My worst fears were being realized: this was an intervention. I held on to my disease with a strength and conviction I felt in no other area of my life, and I wasn't about to give it up. How much did they know?

Quickly, I searched my mental database for any messy clues I might have left behind, things like vile residue on their floors or toilets. I tried to play it cool on the outside even while I was trembling on the inside. I was briefly ecstatic, realizing that none of these friends knew any of the new people I hung out with, many of whom I had manipulated into taking care of my food needs in exchange for a burgeoning friendship. Had my new acquaintances been given the chance to contribute their

Stephanie stories, would I have been checked into the nearest nuthouse?

For three hours they recounted all of my past misdeeds, including breakups, irregular employment, threats of eviction, broken friendships, temporary homelessness, financial instability, and endless stories of other irresponsible behavior. I was drowning in their sea of accusations. But not once did they mention food. Nothing! Nada! What I feared was a serious intervention about my throwing up turned out to be a lecture on every other area my life. Fantastic!

I struggled to maintain a somber composure when what I wanted was to jump up and start dancing the cabbage patch. They didn't suspect I had an eating disorder, which meant I would not have to feign giving it up. But I knew I had to be more careful or eventually I would get caught.

And just like that I felt desperate to begin a binge, but while they were watching me I couldn't take one bite of the food they had laid out. I wondered if I could fix a plate to go. *Focus, Stephanie, focus,* I warned myself. I had to at least pretend to be interested in their ideas to "fix" my life.

"I'm a struggling artist. I don't do things like normal people. I'm different," I protested, even though two of the women in the room were struggling actresses.

"You still have to eat and keep a roof over your head," declared Constance, who had gone the corporate route. "We're always worried about you. You call weeks after disappearing, needing money to pay your rent or some other crazy emergency. Stephanie, you have to grow up. We can't keep enabling you."

Enabling? Hadn't I been financially responsible for myself years earlier than any of them? And even though most addicts in the midst of an intervention would have shut up and ridden it out, I had the nerve to argue. I refused to believe my life was as bad as they said it was.

"Then don't enable me. I don't need any of you doing anything that would make you feel uncomfortable. I have been taking care of myself since I was seventeen, and I can keep taking care of myself." I could feel the swell of defeat pass through my friends as I spoke. Unlike me, they had all had relatively stable upbringings. They could not believe I had survived my childhood, especially since I told my story for dramatic effect. I had learned to use my pain to get attention and to manipulate people into either feeling sorry for me or being impressed by my resilience. The story of my rough childhood was my shield, guarding against suggestions that I grow up and deal. Friends tiptoed around the "get your act together" discussion that any proponent of tough love would have served up cold years ago.

"We're just worried about you," Yvette said. "You were doing so well, and then a couple of years ago, it's like things just started getting bad, and you haven't been able to turn them around." Yvette was an actress who'd done tons of commercials and the occasional television job, but she always kept a waitress gig in case she suddenly found herself otherwise unemployed. She could not understand why I didn't have a plan A, B, and C at the ready in case life proved to be unstable, which in our business meant normal.

These women did not want to further scar me by withholding their friendship and love, but they did inform me in no uncertain terms that I would no longer have access to their pocketbooks. I knew they were worried about me, so I assured them that I would consider going back home and letting my family help me get my life back on track. I left overwhelmed with relief that none of them had busted me on my bulimia.

I had noticed that lately people were less happy to hear from me, and no matter how hard I tried to pretend my life was working, it had become unmanageable. I spent each day chasing a bulimic binge, lying, cheating, manipulating, and stealing from anyone who would allow me even limited access. Everything about me was designed to disguise my inner turmoil and self-loathing: I was attractive, funny, well-spoken, knowledgeable about more useless information than the average person, self-effacing, and had a wit that usually put people at ease. And because I had a junkie sibling, I was aware of the outward signs of addiction and made it a point always to appear in control of myself.

I was not about to give in to the pressure and return to New York defeated, with my ego rammed up my butt. Once again, I became determined to stay in California and deal with my food problems for good.

Like a good little black girl, I turned to religion, first attempting to follow the doctrine espoused by my churchgoing girlfriends. One night I found myself crumbled to the floor on my knees, praying to the God who shows up for people that call out to him only in leap years when things aren't exactly going their way. It wasn't that I didn't believe in the existence of God; I just wasn't sure I would be capable of following the rigid rules I had heard preached during my sisters' and my church visits back in Bed-Stuy. It seemed you had to be good and give up dancing, cursing, drinking, drugs, and sex to not sin, which to me amounted to exorcising anything fun from my life. I'd even met people raised in religions that demanded you not watch television, go to movies, or listen to music because those were ways that the devil got hold of you.

I had always figured I would ride this train of degradation until the wheels came off sometime in my forties or fifties, and only then would I give up my wild ways and settle down to a God-fearing life. Since I'd been on my own, I'd gone to Buddhist shrines, mosques, ashrams, and other places where I believed I could get "God lite," but even the ones that spoke of a universal God demanded some type of commitment in exchange for spiritual rebirth.

But I was desperate, and I needed something to fix me quickly. I could not have my friends thinking I was a mess. And there was another reason I needed to give up my life of "fun." I had to save myself. Even though I still had my sister-

girl hump in the trunk, my body went from emaciated to looking too bloated too often not to have suffered some internal
complications. My puffy cheeks, the raised blood vessels under
my eyes, my bruised knuckles, and my sore throat caused me
to look and feel like the walking dead.

My pattern in the past had been to swear off men and partying and settle into a life anorexic of fun. It would be all work,
work, and more work. Then one day I'd be dragged to a party
or suddenly become interested in a man, and I'd be off to the
races again, straight toward "Happily Never After."

So with all my other options gone I decided that now was
the time to get right with God. I started spending days at the
Self-Realization Fellowship, a Zen Buddhist temple, an ash-
ram, and the Hollywood Church of Religious Science, seeking
an answer that would lead me to sanity. I wanted this God to
heal me immediately, like you see on religious TV. You know,
the shows where people are afflicted with some deadly disorder,
and after meeting some saint they are struck healthy without
any long-term commitment, or strong belief in anything. Yeah,
that was the kind of miracle I wanted. I wanted bulimia to be
a blip on the screen of my life, not this disease that threatened
to ravage me internally and externally, only stopping once all
that remained was a shell of who I used to be.

In the midst of this desire for sanity, after a late-night
binge, I turned on the television. I was riveted when I realized
the movie of the week was *Kate's Secret*, a story about a bulimic
housewife who hides her disease from her family until it almost
kills her. At the end of the show, a public service announcement
offered help options, including information about a twelve-step
program for people with eating disorders. Had I taken even a
moment to think this through, I might have stopped myself,
but I felt motivated by adrenaline and desperation. I also knew
that having the information would be different than using it. It
could be like having a AAA card in case your car breaks down.
You're not planning on using it, but it's there in case of emergency. I knew I needed something to change, and maybe, just

maybe, this could be that solution. I called the operator and got the number and a local meeting list.

I walked into my first twelve-step meeting a few days later. Scared of being alone with food for one more moment, I dragged myself out of my apartment. Once I made the call seeking information, my need to binge and purge went into hyperdrive. It had been three horrific days of bingeing and purging around the clock. No sooner would I finish wiping up the vomit stains on the floor than I would find myself back in the garbage can pulling out discarded binge food. Thoughts of suicide lodged themselves in my brain, and I couldn't stop thinking it would be less painful to end my life than to continue in this hell. But I made a better choice. I got myself to a meeting.

The first thing I noticed when I entered was that the room was full of women who looked nothing like me. The meeting was specifically for anorexics and bulimics, but they were all blonds, brunettes, and redheads, seated alongside the token Asian and Latino. And now me. It looked more like a casting call for a movie about cheerleaders than a somber scene from the movie I had watched a few days earlier. Those people on television appeared ready to jump off bridges, but these girls seemed vibrant and alive, as if they were in Technicolor. I sat as far from them as possible and listened, rooted to my chair, close to the exit in case I felt compelled to bolt. For an hour and a half, I heard stories of pain and rage, sadness and loneliness, hurt and sorrow. But mostly I heard about behavior surrounding food: eating, not eating, starving, overexercising, using laxatives, bingeing, and purging. The women also talked about the food itself: ice cream, cake, doughnuts, pancakes, pizza, chips . . .

I took copious notes whenever a bulimic spoke. But instead of being warned by their versions of hell, I realized I was sitting there searching for better ways to throw up. Only I would view a twelve-step meeting with a food emphasis as "How to Binge and Purge 101."

I was so far away from wanting help. A tiny voice begged me to listen to what these women were saying, to tune in to the familiar tenor of pain in their voices, the hopelessness that had dragged me across this threshold. But my disease had its hooks in me and wasn't interested in letting go. I was powerless and unable to accept even the most subtle suggestion that I needed real help. Sure, I knew that my behavior was far from normal, but I wasn't ready to hear those words from another person, even someone having a similar experience.

When they asked "newcomers" to stand, I refused to budge, even as every eye turned to me, the only chocolate face in a swirl of vanilla. Even now that I had come this far, and despite the difficulty I overcame in forcing myself to the meeting, I again began to question whether I really had a problem. I had not been in an eating-disorder facility. The fact that I did not have health insurance and could not afford it didn't factor into my argument. Compared with some of those women, I could easily convince myself I didn't have a problem. I could get out of bed and socialize with my friends. I had been able to hang on to a job (to a degree), an apartment (to a lesser degree), a man (not my fault). Even trashing myself, bowing and scraping to appease the porcelain goddess, did not convince me I belonged in this room with these women. After all, I was the Strong Black Woman archetype who did not need anything or anybody to survive. I could live on crumbs and air like my ancestors if I had to, and I would survive this, too.

I left that room, hustled to my car, and drove to the nearest doughnut shop, beginning a monster binge. Bulimia for me was temporary, I told myself, and I would stop when I got good and ready, without the help of a bunch of spoiled, rich white women with whom I didn't have anything in common.

Even though I had no faith in the program, I continued to slip into meetings, vanishing before anyone could actually talk to me. I considered it my backup plan, just in case somewhere down the line I discovered that I really did have a serious problem with food. Occasionally I could still have a day or two of normal eating, which always convinced me that all I really needed was more self-control.

But on the darker side, I liked sitting back and feeling superior because, unlike those women, I didn't feel powerless over food, just a bit out of control. I could handle things that others in that room couldn't, and unlike them I didn't need the "higher power" they would talk about as part of the program. I told myself it was a cult, that I knew what a cult felt like from years of watching my mother's involvement in the Communist movement. The group's intention was to change not only my behavior but also me. Sure, the members seemed normal on the outside, but the chants, the traditions, and the prayers, along with the smiling and hugging, were done solely to suck you in. From the moment the meeting started, you were under the group's control—first, you were reminded of the rules, then you heard about someone's experience, strength, and hope; gave money to pay rent for the meeting space; heard other members' three-minute versions of their stories; said a prayer or a poem; and said the closing chant. Finally came the hugging and fellowship. You couldn't just take something away from it; you had to contribute something: yourself. Cults preyed on the vulnerable under the guise of providing solutions to all problems, big and small. Then once you became addicted to the group, they got you to invite more people, and before you knew it you had no life, and everything you ever desired was tossed aside in favor of satisfying the needs of the cult.

I had never been a joiner; even in high school I befriended kids from most groups—stoners, jocks, preppies, nerds, homies—without ever committing to any of them. I had a natural suspicion of anything organized that could be separated into categories of us and them. I was like a two-year-old stomping my feet, demanding I do things my way.

Within months, I hit a new low with bulimia. I once again moved back to New York. I had decided that being at home would allow me to get to the root of my problem, dig it up, and start all over. For years I thought of L.A. as the origination point of my bulimia, and therefore the place where I would find a cure. But it had become clear—perhaps from what I'd been hearing in meetings—that my issues with food began way back in childhood. They were there inside of me, which is where I had to start searching if I ever wanted to get better.

I tried the twelve-step meetings in New York, but they weren't like those in Los Angeles, where you could find many meetings specifically for anorexics and bulimics. And unlike Los Angeles meetings, which felt like an extension of high school, with people forming cliques and pairing off after the meeting to head to the local vegetarian restaurant or yogurt shop, New Yorkers usually came and left alone. They wanted their recovery to be like their lives: independent and anonymous. While I wasn't comfortable with the kissy-huggy-live-on-my-couch-until-you-get-abstinent codependency of Los Angeles meetings, I rarely felt an ounce of warmth in the New York rooms. These people had no interest in my song and dance. While the members in both places took their abstinence seriously, it just looked and felt different.

On the subway one day, my arms clutching a bagful of bagels, my body anxious with anticipation of that first bite, I flipped to the back of the *Village Voice*. There in bold print was an ad that caught my attention: "If you suffer from bulimia, we may be able to help you." Right there in writing was the kind of quick-fix solution I had been searching for. Nothing in the advertisement said anything about changing, and it certainly didn't suggest you go through twelve steps. There was noth-ing like the fourth step, taking a searching and fearless moral inventory of yourself. Nor did it talk about a ninth step, mak-ing amends to all those you had harmed. In fact, it didn't even suggest you take the first step by admitting you were powerless over food.

This would be my solution. My cure. When I got home I dialed the number desperate to be done with this food addiction.

Four days later, I traveled to the respected teaching hospi-tal and registered in the guinea-pig program intended to cure bulimics. For two hours, a series of wet-behind-the-ears Ph.D. candidates grilled me about my mental, physical, and emo-tional health.

Were you physically abused by either of your parents?
How many times a day do you throw up?
Do you hate yourself?
Do you have a trigger food?

The questions were endless. When a doctor interviewed me, his colleagues kept appearing in the doorway as if I were some curiosity.

He apologized for his coworkers' lack of professionalism. "You're the first African American applicant we've had in the program," he explained.

"I binge and purge just like every other bulimic," I assured him. I wondered if I should have confessed to bingeing on fried chicken and cornbread so he'd be able to find comfort in a stereotype.

During my next session he handed me a bottle of pills, directing me to take one each day at the same time. I was informed that some patients received real medication, while others were given a placebo. None of the patients knew who received the actual drugs.

After months of filling out questionnaires and taking med-ication that usually wound up in the toilet after a binge, I realized these doctors did not have a magical cure for me, especially not in pill form. And I was sick and tired of being their guinea pig.

After a three-day bender of bingeing and purging with no relief in sight, I took a sharp razor out of the medicine cabinet and sliced my tongue until it bled. After the first few slices I kept cutting, hoping to mutilate my desire to binge. I hoped the pain of a stinging tongue would make me forget about food for at least a day. I only wanted twenty-four hours of relief. It had been so long since I had been able to gather the strength to stop eating compulsively for even one day.

Two hours later, nothing could deter me from yet another binge, and I was off again. My tongue felt like it had been lit on fire. I wanted to drink pitchers of water or place ice cubes in my mouth to stop the pain, except I couldn't. Too much liquid made it impossible to bring up the food. It would only allow a few swimming particles to resurface. I had to suffer the pain in order to have my binge.

Usually, I entered a binge in a trancelike state, as though sleepwalking, but the pain of my tongue didn't allow that. It forced me to be present.

In that moment, my red, raw tongue bulging from the cuts looked like a raw cut of meat, just as I expected my insides would look if I were allowed to cut myself open and take a peek. Would this be my addiction bottom?

Part Three

After

Giving Up the Fight

After going to half a dozen meetings in New York over a six-month period, I realized that I would never get abstinent in those rooms. I could not even stand up and admit that I had a problem. I also realized I needed to get far away from my family if I was going to dig to the bottom of my dysfunction and my issues. Home might be where the heart is, but it wasn't a place where I felt comfortable splaying myself open to reveal my deepest wounds.

I convinced a friend to buy me a one-way plane ticket back to Los Angeles. Once more, my life had become unmanageable, and once more I was emotionally and mentally spent. Every day I became more like a hamster on a wheel, fighting to keep from falling off, never really getting anywhere.

I had gained enough insight to know that to survive, to become human again, I had to stop gobbling down my shame; I had to turn it outward and expose it to the light. I could present it on a silver platter, give it the audience it deserved, and in that process I might find buried underneath it the little girl who wanted to die, who used this disease to numb a lifetime of pain. In my exhaustion, I could no longer pretend to be normal like the rest of the world, those who knew how to eat, how to laugh, how to love deeply without reservation or self-consciousness. I had spent so much time shooting down my needs, scared of being singled out as the weak one. Attending meetings had not made me abstinent, particularly since I hadn't done one thing they suggested. But in spite of myself I became more self-aware. How could I not? Hearing the heart-wrenching stories of other women's struggles with food and themselves had a real impact on me. Finally I had come to realize that love from others would never fix this. I first had to learn how to love myself. But I did not have a clue how to start.

On my first Monday back in Los Angeles I crawled into a meeting for bulimics and anorexics, desperate to take the first step and state aloud that I was powerless over my relationship with food. As much as I hated to admit that I needed this group of mostly middle-class and rich white women, I had no choice. I had tried everything else. I had begun to take action, doing some of the things that scared me, including showing up at this meeting when I would rather have been at home with my head in the toilet.

I had heard in a meeting back in New York that the definition of "insanity" is doing the same thing repeatedly and expecting a different result. So this time, instead of sitting in the back, I parked my butt in a seat up front.

I sat there, frozen, a melanin-enriched alien, as an assortment of Daddy's girls whined about their inability to stop throwing up or starving themselves to death. My skin crawled as they described their addictions, some details mirroring my own. Their talks ripped a hole in my ghetto-girl beliefs that money solved any and all problems. How many times had I blamed my bulimia on poverty? *If only I didn't have to worry about money* had become my prebinge mantra. It made throwing up my food circumstantial and not my fault. Nothing was ever my fault.

Now, however, not only was I in a meeting, but I was sitting up front and finally willing to listen. That day, in that one meeting, many of my sister-outsider reasons for throwing up were shot to hell. I soon learned that privileged girls raised by two well-educated, wealthy, attentive parents could still find themselves facedown in toilets fighting for their lives. The reasons we all threw up were diverse and multifaceted: low self-esteem, social pressure, childhood molestation, anxiety, rage . . .

After that meeting I fled to the safety of my car, certain I'd never return, but eventually I did just that. What choice did I have? Where else could I find a roomful of women and the occasional man fighting to abstain from my same addiction and willing to talk about it? So return I did, hovering on the fringe until the day when I stood up on the podium and began to share my story.

That first time I stood at the mic, I nervously spoke about the isolation of being a poor black woman fighting bulimia. I had never spoken those words aloud to another living soul, and here I was standing up in a room of white women. It was hard not to feel like I had just relinquished my black card with that simple action, but silence and isolation had become my enemies. Returning to my seat I felt self-conscious and raw. I had never allowed myself to be that vulnerable before, and I'd become so used to hiding my real feelings that I did not even know I could access them that easily. But pride was my new emotion, because finally I had told the truth.

Immediately after me, a tall, lithe, well-dressed blond stepped forward. Her words threatened to eject me from the room forever.

Fighting back tears, she began, "I don't understand why I am slowly, surely, trying to kill myself by throwing up. I have a great life, and I have never wanted for anything. My parents pay my rent and buy me a new BMW every year because they want me to drive a safe car. I wish I were a poor black woman because then maybe this need to throw up my life would make sense."

All eyes widened and swiveled in my direction, igniting my feelings of shame and rage. The twelve-step rule of "No cross talk," meaning members cannot comment on others' stories, had been broken across my backside, and I wanted blood. Glaring at the woman, I told myself that she couldn't last a day living my life.

After the meeting, as I attempted a swift disappearance out the door, the lead speaker caught up with me. "Please," she said, "keep coming back and I promise you it will work."

I left the meeting that night, my car pointed in the direction of home, and I began yet another epic and committed binge lasting hours, until my jaws tired of chewing and not even green bile rose up in my throat. The next morning I awoke hungover from the binge the night before, feeling worse than I had in a long time.

It was the first time I believed that there was a way out of this hell that had become a poor substitute for my life. I was finally willing to take that first step and admit that I was powerless over food . . . at least I thought I was willing.

At the next meeting I raised my hand when they asked for newcomers, and I kept going to that meeting every Monday. Each Sunday night I'd wind up sitting on my hands, begging myself to stay abstinent for just one more day so that I could share my success in the meeting. No matter how hard I white-knuckled it, I couldn't stop throwing up.

But I had begun to feel less isolated. Instead of allowing my life to revolve around food, I started letting it revolve around my recovery, and that meant "program," which I had learned was how insiders referred to the twelve steps. I befriended a couple of other newcomers, and together we committed to going to meetings. They became my lifeline. I totally checked out of my life of substituting addiction for recovery. There didn't seem to be any way to do this part-time. I could tell these women if I was about to binge or call them after I finished a binge, something I would never do with my other friends, and they never made me feel judged or fucked up. In fact my program buddies treated me much better than I treated myself. But I also treated them better than myself, too.

There was a saying, "We will love you until you can love yourself," but I did not see how that was possible. None of these women really knew me. They had no idea what terrible things I had done in order to keep throwing up. They didn't know the dark secrets that made me turn to food in the first place—so forgive me for being skeptical. I didn't know how any of them could relate to me growing up hungering for love, physical affection, and food. Or how those desires got all confused and jumbled around in my brain like scrambled eggs. And how would any of them be able to relate to my life as a poor, illegitimate child in Brooklyn?

I started to see that most of my initial issues with joining a group or becoming a part of anything had much to do with my transient upbringing. Whenever I'd allow myself to get close to anyone or to get comfortable at a school, we moved or I changed schools. Change was the only familiar theme in my childhood. If there was one thing I was sure about as a girl, it was that my life could change at any moment; maybe not today or tomorrow, but as soon as my mother lost interest in how our current life was going, we were off to the next destination. So even though logic told me program would not change, holding back my commitment was so second nature that it went beyond common sense and evidence.

I went to a bunch of meetings, but my favorites were the ones with an emphasis on bulimia and anorexia. There I felt camaraderie. We had all done the same things to maintain the secrecy of our disease; we'd all stolen money, eaten out of garbage cans, stolen food, lied to checkout clerks about our junk-food groceries, and driven miles out of our way to buy binge food, losing jobs, friends, boyfriends, and our self-esteem in the process. And as much as I hated this new "program life," I couldn't control my addiction without it.

I met a couple of other black girls at meetings; they were both upper-middle class. One had the distinct aura of *I want to be the only black girl in the room,* so I kept my distance from her. The other became an occasional program buddy. Later, as I became more comfortable admitting my eating disorder, many sister-girlfriends admitted to also being bulimic and anorexic, and I'd encourage them to seek help, but they were unwilling to share their shame in public.

Over the years, I would meet a bunch of other black girls who did come to a meeting, but rarely would they stay. I'd run into some of them at church or out at get-togethers, but they usually didn't come back to the meetings. Most chose not to share their private issues in a room full of white girls, but that choice had been made for me—I needed program.

One of the suggestions in the twelve steps is that you get a sponsor, someone who has what you want—usually abstinence from your addiction—and a shared history. Other bulimics and anorexics explained that someday at a meeting I would hear my story out of someone else's mouth and that the person telling it should be my sponsor. Watching the sponsors and their sponsees gathering after meetings was like one of those connection exercises you do in preschool, where you draw a line between objects and their owners: fire hat connects to the fireman; police whistle connects to the policewoman, etc. Anorexics were usually sponsored by former anorexics whose bodies still managed to be slightly thinner than normal. Bulimics tended to go toward the recovered bulimic who managed to keep her body together but could be a little thicker and whose weight still tended to fluctuate. Compulsive overeaters tended to sponsor compulsive overeaters who were heavier. That's not how it worked for me.

The first sponsor I chose could not have been further from me, but she had a hard-core abstinence, and that's what I needed to save my life. It's not just that she wasn't black. I had long since given up expecting a sponsor with dark skin and kinky hair and a complicated family tree. Her story bore little to no resemblance to mine, and her body—at five feet two inches and about one hundred forty-five pounds—was not even close, because at five-five, I rarely slipped over one hundred twenty pounds. But she was a recovered alcoholic and ex-bulimic who worked her program like a boot camp and had a twenty-year abstinence from both alcohol and bulimia. The last thing I cared about at this point was the size of her butt.

She had toughness like my mother, which I found familiar and comforting. My tendency was to be hardheaded, and I needed someone who wasn't going to let me charm my way out of taking action. Plus, I was able to manipulate with a sob story that made people open their homes, wallets, and hearts before they knew it. I needed tough love and not the wishy-washy connect-with-you-inner-child version I had seen between many sponsors and sponsees. She also had control over her addiction and wasn't obsessing about her body, and what I wanted above all else was that kind of control.

By the way, that first step—recognizing a powerlessness over your disease and giving up control—hadn't fully penetrated yet, although I would quickly argue that it had. Rome wasn't built in a day, and neither could I become a healthy, happy, and sane person so easily.

I had arrived at the point where I knew my disease wasn't about the food. My sponsor not only insisted that I attend thirty meetings in thirty days, but she also insisted that I volunteer, making coffee, setting up chairs, selling literature, calling newcomers, and so on. She helped me learn how to eat abstinently because I hadn't been able to get a handle on my food. Eating three meals a day hadn't happened for me in a long time. My eating had been closer to one meal that lasted all day, or thirty meals a day. I didn't know how to stop eating once I started, and she was helping me relearn this.

At first I had a lot of shame at not being able to control my relationship with food without this help, but that was before I truly understood that for me food was not just sustenance, it was my coping mechanism. Food was what I used to cope with hurt and shame and pain and fear and insecurity and any other feeling of discomfort that I experienced. My thought had always been, *Depressed?* Eat a doughnut. *Sad?* Have some popcorn. *Lonely?* Ice cream will fix it. *Feeling critical?* Nothing goes better with low self-esteem than candy. Anger required something hard and crunchy, which usually meant potato chips.

I used food the same way others used heroin or cocaine or alcohol or other drugs. However, a friend who used to be obese explained how difficult it had been for her to get abstinent because unlike drugs, which addicts give up completely, you still need to eat to stay alive. Heroin isn't readily available at the drugstore or supermarket or drive-thru. People don't randomly phone with offers for heroin dates, and in most circles you can't socialize while using your drug of choice in public. Most social activities don't revolve around drugs; they revolve around eating.

I couldn't maintain abstinence alone. My sponsor strongly suggested that I begin to bookend my meals with her. This meant that I'd call her before a meal and tell her exactly what I planned to eat and how much, and then I'd call when I finished so that my meal didn't continue for hours. I felt like a four-year-old, but at least I was a four-year-old who wasn't throwing up.

Through this simple exercise, I learned the power of honesty. I understood that if I lied to my sponsor about what I ate, I would feel bad, and that would affect my ability to remain abstinent. So many of the last few years had been spent lying in order to keep practicing my eating disorder that now I had to catch myself from telling even the whitest lies. I had grown used to lying about everything.

Many of my core issues came out in my relationship with food. I started to see that by lying I was avoiding intimacy, so that ultimately I'd never form a real bond and run the risk of needing people and being vulnerable. My sponsor listened to me daily and pointed out my pattern of making changes in my story for no reason at all. The process took patience on her side, but never once did I feel judged or crazy.

And I learned to tell the truth. She taught me to treat myself like a baby and to remember that so much of my recovery was about teaching that baby how to take care of herself and how to grow up. As someone who always assumed I knew more than most people, I had a hard time allowing myself to be vulnerable and patient with myself and to need others.

My sponsor saw that I was having a hard time wrapping my mind around this foreign practice of being gentle with myself and brought it to my attention. Gentleness was not a part of my upbringing, and so I didn't trust it. The simple truth was that I didn't know how to be gentle with myself without feeling weak. Weakness was one emotion that scared me, but the other key emotion was anger. Unlike my mother, whom I'd grown up seeing uncontrollably angry all the time, I shoved my anger down, refusing to acknowledge its existence. I saw anger as a violent, consuming emotion that left no room for its opposite, love, and that terrified me. I equated my mother's anger with her inability to attract love. To me anger was a shield that kept all good things—love, success, fun, and happiness—from entering your life.

At first I rebelled and tried desperately to hold on to control and toughness while maintaining my abstinence, but it didn't work. It almost led me back into the toilet. I wanted to be emotionally removed, tough, and independent like the other women in my family, forgetting how many of them had suffered from depression and suicidal thoughts. That thinking kept me from fully committing to my recovery.

One day I went out to eat with my "normal" friends. In a crowd, I always pretended that I could eat whatever I wanted and be OK. I hadn't yet told any of them that I had an eating disorder or that I was attending meetings.

But I felt physically and emotionally unable to sit there with food digesting in my stomach. Everything they did and said after that first bite became a fog as I drifted in and out of consciousness and the conversation. Pretending to be normal led to self-loathing, which led to overeating, which led to extreme discomfort, and all I wanted was to be facedown in the toilet puking out my guts.

But I had come so far. I had already logged thirty consecutive days of abstinence from throwing up. Did I really want to start over? To tell my program friends that I had slipped and fallen back into the food because of my ego?

I sat there stuck between the two realities, the food and my friends, and I felt so scared and helpless that I got up, went into the bathroom, dropped down on my knees, and began to pray. I said the twelve-step prayer over and over: *God, grant me the serenity to accept the things I cannot change, courage to change the things that I can, and wisdom to know the difference.* I kneeled there for what felt like an eternity, time enough to purge a bunch of times, but instead I just prayed. A new stillness washed over me, replacing my anxiety and fear. Suddenly I knew I would be OK. I would survive this disease for today.

I had always looked for the quick fixes, but now my life got really simple, and I began to live one day at a time, one meal at a time, one minute at a time. I didn't care if I wasn't popular or skinny or funny. I stopped fearing that my personality would go through a lobotomy, that I would become unrecognizable, that all facets of my individuality would wash away. I knew that there were other ways—girlfriends had gotten abstinent in inpatient facilities, outpatient hospitals, through diet centers, getting saved, and just praying—but I hadn't found another way that I could afford or that worked. I hadn't discovered a magical pill to end my need to throw up my life or a man who made me permanently lose my appetite for bingeing and purging. The only way I knew to get over my food addiction was to finish what I'd started, to do the work, and to feel my feelings. That sucked for someone like me, but I had no choice. I was truly humbled, brought to my knees, but the thing I discovered in those moments was that I wanted a life, a real life with a career and a mate and a safe car and money in the bank and a healthy, happy future.

I stopped fighting recovery and committed my life to the twelve-step program 24-7. With the help of my sponsor and new friends, I managed to keep my abstinence. And it wasn't easy. I had spent so many years blaming my circumstances for my problems: *If I only had enough money to go away to college. If only I were able to pay my rent. If only I had a father who loved me.* It had never occurred to me that the reasons my life had become so unmanageable could have anything to do with me or that I rarely took responsibility for my choices.

Having finally experienced a degree of abstinence, I never wanted to go back to a life of bulimic insanity. I wanted this new freedom and new happiness that were promised in the big book of Alcoholics Anonymous (every addiction program uses the same book). I wanted to like the me staring back in the mirror every day instead of wincing when I saw my reflection because I couldn't stop remembering all the terrible things I had done in my life or the people I had hurt and lied to in order to afford my addiction.

And so instead of using the program as a stopgap measure until I could figure out how to get healthy without growing or changing or taking any responsibility, I dove all the way in.

When I got to the God part of program, I found I had years of doubt and anger to overcome before I could believe that a power greater than myself could restore me to sanity. At around seven years old, I stopped believing in Santa Claus and God all at once and decided to grow up. Maybe there was a Santa Claus, but he couldn't access our apartment since there were no fireplaces in tenement buildings in Bed-Stuy. Perhaps he had tried to shove food and clothing and the rare toy under our door to ensure we'd have a merry Christmas but failed because nothing would fit. Whatever! I didn't care what the excuse was.

And I felt the same about God, a gigantic disappointment who never managed to deliver anything I prayed for no matter what deals I made, including promises to behave and to stop causing trouble. God gave only to those he had deemed worthy, like the Brady Bunch on television, and they weren't like me. They were lily white with perfect lives and a maid to pick up after them. But on *Good Times* the Evans family lived in the projects and was always praying just to keep the lights on. And this God everybody raved about didn't appear too kind to my family either. He didn't protect me from nightmares and monsters and an empty stomach. So why should I put my limited faith in some entity who never showed up on my block?

My sponsor explained that I didn't need to believe in a specific God to achieve abstinence; some people made their "higher power" the ocean or the trees or the sky or the sun, while others even referred to their "higher power" as the absence of God.

A psychic had once told me, "Stephanie, if you see an easy path and a harder path, you will always take the difficult path. If you go to the beach and the tide goes out, you will jump up and down screaming, 'The tide went out, the tide went out' instead of taking a book and getting comfortable and relaxing because you realize that the tide going out is a temporary and often necessary part of the cycle of life." He continued, "If you allow yourself to trust that even though the tide went out, it will eventually come back in, you will enjoy the experience, and it will lack drama."

Little did I know then that I needed drama in my life to wave over everything like a big smoke screen. With drama I didn't have to focus inward on myself. Drama forced people to see exactly what I wanted them to see: *My ex was bisexual so of course I wasn't enough for him, but please pass me the tissues as I sob uncontrollably because I loved him. . . . I didn't realize he had a girlfriend. I love him. . . .* And so on.

Suddenly I was exposing all my feelings, failings, vulnerabilities, and fuck-ups. I had no one and nothing to blame but myself. I had been a mess for a long time, covering it up, disguising it with wit and drama. But now those trappings were removed, and I had to stand in the moment and watch as the tide went out in my life. I had exhausted myself jumping up and down, yelling and screaming, so that a crowd would gather around my life and point at the drama. I was tired of hiding.

I came to believe in God in a way I never had before. I had always thought God existed only for those who led a righteous life or at least believed they did. Until one day at a bulimarexic meeting a manorexic stood up to share his story. He explained his lifelong discomfort with the concept of God. And even though there is no cross talk in meetings, I had to stop myself from being a part of his amen corner. He had been raised to think that the only God who existed was one who dangled his acceptance like a carrot, always just a bit out of reach. His sponsor had explained to him that his higher power did not have to be the same God of his childhood. He said, "I asked my sponsor would it be OK if my higher power was Michael Jordan, because when he goes to the basket, odds are that he is going to make the shot. That is the kind of God I wanted, one who allowed me to always take another shot, having faith that eventually I would make it into the basket. So my God is Michael Jordan."

Even though I am not a sports fan and I didn't want my God to be anyone I knew, I also couldn't tie my faith to someone in the sky looking down on me demanding that I live a perfect life now so that I could be rewarded in the next. My sponsor suggested I write a help-wanted ad for a God, describing all the characteristics I wanted in him or her. My list included compassion, love, acceptance, humor, and a list of other things, ending with not making me blow up and get fat. Over time my list changed until the God that I asked the universe for is the one that now I believe in.

In order to truly grasp the magnitude of my ability to love and accept God, you have to first understand I'd spent my life hating him.

I had always had such disdain for addicts of any kind that getting into acceptance about my own disease proved particularly difficult. Years later I remember talking to my sister Cecilia, who lay dying in a hospice from ovarian cancer and AIDS, about her drug abuse. Her impending death tore down all the walls we (mostly I) had built up against each other and smashed us close. Death made it impossible to talk around things and demanded that we skip straight to the point. We had daily phone calls that helped us to heal. For the first and last time in her life we had a real talk about her addiction to crack cocaine. Before program I had placed myself on a pedestal high above the gutter my junkie sister called home. I had no compassion or patience for her experiences in childhood, even though many of them mirrored my own. My sensitive sister didn't have the thick skin or resiliency I depended on to pull me through crises. It took a long time for me to be able to see that my sister and I were two little brown girls who didn't get their needs met, born to another brown girl who didn't get her needs met, who was born to another brown girl who didn't get her needs met.

Bulimia was a serious addiction, but much of it had to do with hiding in plain sight. The best thing about my eating disorder was that it didn't show. I didn't get too skinny or too fat. I didn't smell from the stench of alcohol or scratch from the desire for more heroin. There were no obvious signs as to why my life had spiraled out of control; so as far as anyone could tell, I was unlucky or untalented or unmotivated or uninterested in a better life but what I wasn't was a messy, feigning, lying, cheating, stealing addict. But of course I was. With bulimia I had fooled them all, and for a long while I even lied to myself that my disease was nothing compared to my sister's. Renee used to try to teach me to be compassionate with Cecilia, but I had no patience. "She's a loser," I'd respond when Renee asked me to give her a call or a chance. "It's disgusting." I'd turn up my nose, desperate to distance myself from my sister who stole from everybody. I didn't want her dark, troubled shadow to fall on me. So I hid my sister from my friends, obliterated her from family history, and kept her pictures hidden. But after I entered program I came to understand that the reason I didn't have compassion for Cecilia was that I didn't have any compassion for myself. She reminded me too much of myself, and I was unwilling to find any comparison.

But as my sister lay dying we were able to talk, to really communicate about all the things we knew we weren't going to have a chance to discuss later. For her there would be no later. I wanted to know mostly if she had any regrets about the path she had taken, about the drug-induced life that had led her to this certain ending. "I know why I got high. Life is too damn painful. It hurts a lot, and I would rather get high than feel that kind of pain. I don't know how people do it," she told me. That was so much confirmation about choice. My entire family had rallied at some point or another to help my sister get clean and sober. They helped put her into rehab facilities or took her in, even moved her to a different state to keep her clean. And in twenty-five years nothing could keep her sober, because no matter what she said, she didn't want to give up drugs.

In program I heard people say that until you are sick and tired of being sick and tired, you won't change. In twenty-five years my sister never got sick and tired of being a junkie, and if she could have she would have used drugs until the day she died. But unlike my sister I was way beyond sick and tired, and so I took my fourth step and made a searching and fearless moral inventory. At this point in my life if someone had told me that shaving off my hair and dancing and singing Hare Krishna songs on Venice Beach would guarantee my abstinence forever, I might have leapt at the commune life.

The Inward Journey

The havoc I had wreaked on my life was massive. Acknowledging the damage I had done was essential to my healing process, although looking at all the ways in which I'd supported my addiction would prove harder than becoming abstinent. A searching and fearless moral inventory of my past felt impossible, but my sponsor believed in tough love, and that's exactly what I needed. I knew that I was a low-bottom addict and that, had I been able to maintain any semblance of sanity, I would have surely continued along my path of destruction until the bitter end, just like my sister.

My sponsor suggested I get a composition notebook and start at what I remembered as the beginning. By this point in my life, I had done so many horrible things that I wondered if this meant going back to the age of seven, when I intentionally told my cousin he was getting a bike for his birthday and ruined his surprise. Did this mean age two, when I caused so much drama because I refused to eat my oatmeal at breakfast, and when my aunt yelled, "Child, eat that oatmeal!" I responded curtly that I was not her child?

"How far back is this beginning?" I finally asked her.

"As early as you feel you have to go to get it all out," she said.

She then explained I should envision my mind and body as vessels that I'd spent years filling up with negativity, hurt, anger, pain, lies, and . . . well, let's just say the list is long. I should see myself as a vessel filled with shit (yes, manure, crap), and every time I faced up to a new truth, I would be scooping out some of that waste, making room for more light, joy, and goodness. It was bad things out, good things in.

I wanted so much to be filled with light and love and to be done with guilt and shame and low self-esteem. I was so tired of feeling bad about myself while putting on a loud show to prove to others how great I was. I couldn't wait to experience a new freedom and a new happiness.

When I finally wrote down on paper all the terrible things I had done in order to practice my disease, I almost stuck my head back in the toilet. There it was on the lined pages—every awful thing I had done, including some I'd tried to erase from my memory. I had never faced my own shame, and holding a mirror up to my actions and seeing their ugliness made me understand why I'd wanted to kill myself all those years ago. But it also finally made me grateful that I hadn't, because I had people in my life who had gone through this journey with me and were able to love and accept me as I walked along that path to wholeness. They were available 24-7 to help me face myself.

A side benefit of reviewing my past was that I became more honest. I admitted to myself that even in meetings, where you are given three minutes to share your experience, strength, and hope with fellow addicts, I had always chosen what version of my story to share based on my audience.

Do I need to be perceived as a victim today? I'd think, and that would lead to a more devastating version of my story.

Were there young women in the audience to whom I had made outreach calls? Well, that required the strong, proud, I-can-get-through-anything version.

Because I constantly found myself in new environments as a kid, it became second nature to me to size up my audience before deciding what version of myself I needed to be. These differing personas were never out-and-out lies, just distorted variations on the same theme: a colorfully messed-up childhood. Now I finally came to understand that my life had only one version.

I took another huge step toward health and away from addiction when, against my family's vocal protests that "only crazy people go to head shrinkers," I began therapy. I especially needed to be heard. The first thing my therapist pointed out to me was my inability to live in the gray area of life. Everything was either black or white for me, good or bad, happy or depressed. I was starting to see that when I couldn't pay my rent, a suicide attempt was not exactly a normal response. I had to learn to give up my need to be happy all the time.

Much time passed before I was able to stop that raging voice of my mother in my head, yelling, "What are you upset about? I'm the one who has to get up, go to work, and support three children!"

Being unhappy had always felt like a betrayal of my mother's efforts—working jobs where she wasn't treated the way she deserved or paid decently in order to provide for us—so I had nowhere to put those feelings, leaving me to beat myself up, eventually choosing the ultimate abuse of bulimia.

Saying I threw up my life for just one reason would be too easy, since I could quickly come up with a dozen reasons. And although all of the reasons would be true, alone they still wouldn't be enough.

I also needed to forgive myself for being bulimic, for being molested, for feeling like a burden, and for loads of other things I used against myself to destroy my self-esteem. Every time I took care of myself, ate healthy, talked about my fear instead of hiding, helped someone else in need, or paid my bills on time, I grew stronger, and food became less and less important—not in the anorexic's controlling way but by using food to nurture my body and to keep me healthy. Food became what it was meant to be—sustenance.

As I grew stronger, I started to share my experience, strength, and hope not just at meetings but also at colleges. I found that by telling my most shameful secrets to young women still struggling with food, bulimia lost its power over me. Bringing my disease into the light relieved me of my shame instead of increasing it.

But the biggest difference was that as I started to own my feelings of low self-esteem, sadness, rage, anger, and insecurity, the pain began to lift. Memories of childhood came flooding back, along with the feelings I had buried. Suddenly I experienced sadness that did not make me slump into feelings of suicide, and joy no longer made me change my entire life on a whim. I also was able to remember all the great things about my childhood and my mother that had gotten tossed aside after the rape. I took back my happy memories and allowed myself to enjoy them. I stopped being so hard on myself; instead I accepted myself as human.

And in accepting myself as human, I admitted that, contrary to my atheist upbringing, I needed a spiritual practice and a higher power, a God to call my own and a community where I could worship and find peace. I joined a Church and started to take classes, including one called Self-Mastery. I went on silent meditation retreats, taking as many opportunities as possible to go inward and to be alone. I practiced daily meditation and journaling.

I developed a yearning to give back, and I began to do regular volunteer work. I had always felt sorry for myself when looking back at my past, resenting the lack and limitations, always diving into one pity party after another. I had been an expert at feeling sorry for myself. But I learned that the best way to stay abstinent is by helping others. There was a saying in the program: "You can't keep it if you don't give it away." I found an unexpected bonus: helping others made me feel worthy, that I had something of value to offer in the world.

As a consequence of loving myself I began to love my family, to accept them for who they are, and to understand that most of them had always loved me in their own way. I reached out to my mother and stopped blaming her for failing to give me what I needed in childhood. I understood that even though she had done things differently than I would have liked, she did the very best she could with what she had.

I also appreciated where I came from, no longer hiding behind it like a victim. I found strength in the way my family had survived on so little. How they never turned away anyone in need, no matter how little they had to share.

I forgave them for not being psychic about my rape and not protecting me from my uncle. Forgiving myself made room for me to forgive others. I wasn't perfect, and I stopped expecting others to be perfect. I gave up being pissed off at the circumstances of my birth and saw my life as a miracle. I stopped thinking it was an accident that I had been born into my family, and I began to count my blessings.

Unlike the miracle cure I wanted, leaving my bulimia behind proved to be good old-fashioned hard work. Despite my best efforts, there was no quick recovery. Once I stopped throwing up, I began to gain weight, and my body clung to every new pound, afraid I would start to starve myself again. I could do nothing as the pounds came on, and I could no longer hide my food issues. I didn't blow up as I had feared. But because body dysmorphic syndrome made me see my body differently than it was, any weight gain felt substantial. Ten newly gained pounds felt like fifty.

But as painful as it was to watch my body stretch out of my control, I couldn't turn back to the food. Instead of running around and filling my time with people in order to get away from myself, I began to seek solitude. I gave up acting, admitting that it had never truly been my dream. I even stopped dating, needing to be OK with myself before I tried to merge heart first with another person. Instead of romance novels, I now read all kinds of books on God and peace and self-reliance. Instead of looking for the hottest party, I would go to the bookstore and drink tea, reading books that offered strength, guidance, and spiritual growth. Sundays I went to church. I learned how to meditate, to sit alone with my thoughts, and to quiet my mind. I had spent so much time chasing fabulous, wanting to be a part of something larger and more exciting than me. Being alone before had always meant isolation, abandonment, punishment, and now I craved it.

Everything about me changed, but because this was something I was doing to get my own attention, and not the attention of my friends or the latest guy I liked, it felt effortless, and I barely noticed it happening. In the words of my close friend Billie Williams Neal, I was becoming more myself. I no longer craved the full attention of the world. I wanted simply to know myself and to heal.

Becoming more introspective was just the beginning. Continuing to follow the specific steps of program, I went to each and every person I had harmed and laid out in exact detail what I had done—lying, stealing, everything. Most of my friends immediately forgave me, although I still was not convinced I deserved forgiveness. A few took this as an opportunity to end the friendship, preferring less drama in their lives. As much as it hurt to feel abandoned, I understood people wanting to have friendships that they could trust.

My abstinence could be summed up in two words: "growing up." Because I had supported myself since the age of seventeen I had always assumed that I was mature for my age and ahead of my peers. After all, I had been self-reliant for years prior to and occasionally during my addiction. My family never had the means to rescue me from debt, to offer a financial solution to my problems, or to help me overcome any emotional issues. From an early age I took care of it all myself. Not to mention that I had been referred to as "wise for my age" since I had been ejected from my mother's womb. For me, this was tangible proof of maturity.

But once I took stock of my life, I discovered that when my attention was focused outward, all of my anger and my negative feelings were trapped within. If anyone ever pointed to me and said I was lacking self-esteem, I would call the person a hater. Couldn't people tell by my diction, my clothing, and my bold air of confidence that the last thing I lacked was self-esteem? *Nobody ever loved herself more than I do* was the underlying message of most of my conversations.

That was my spiel before I began to delve into my core issues, and then I could barely stand myself. The lie that I had been living, featuring myself as the fabulous star of this hard-core drama called life, was blown wide open. At a meeting I once heard a speaker refer to herself as "the piece of shit that the world revolved around." That was something I heard often to describe addicts—self-involved people with no self-esteem who needed everything to center on them, and I was no different. I was that piece of shit!

In being honest with myself and others, I started to look forward to each day. People no longer had the look of trapped rats when they saw me coming, wondering what I needed from them this time. I stopped borrowing money from people—no matter what my circumstances. If I needed something, I had to earn the money myself to buy it. And money, that magical thing that I held in high esteem and believed would make me worthy and lovable, dropped from my top-ten list. Sure, I wanted money; I needed it in order to survive. But I no longer saw it as the best solution to healing my poor childhood.

On Solid Ground

Today my life feels as if it has come full circle because now I am the mother. Like me as a child, my daughter Zoë does not have a big appetite and is a picky eater. She eats when she is hungry, but I believe that because both her father and I provide her with physical and emotional expressions of love, food is not a hot-button issue for her. Although I am divorced from her father, we coparent successfully and work together so that her needs always come first. We attend her recitals, softball and soccer games, parent-teacher conferences, and doctor visits together, and we discuss the constant care and feeding of Zoë. To her, the world is a magical place where all her needs are met and her parents double as short-order cooks, chauffeurs, entertainers, and personal shoppers. When she finds herself upset because something does not go her way, usually in the play-date/more-ice-cream realm, she comes to me and says, "Mommy, I'm not happy." Even though she is eight, and I could give her a quick fix, I choose not to sugarcoat the truth.

"Zoë," I say, "nobody can be happy all the time. Besides, if you are never sad how will you know what happiness feels like?" I'd be lying if I said this went over well.

I know that what she wants in that moment is permission to run next door and play with the neighbor or to have that second serving of ice cream, but it is important to me that my daughter learns how to navigate through her feelings of unhappiness. It is imperative to me as a mother that my child is able to feel her feelings even if they are "horrible"—her word, not mine. As a child I was never allowed to be sad, mad, or upset. I had to be in a perpetual state of "OK" in order for my mother to feel like she was doing a decent job of raising my sisters and me, and it made me unable to handle negative feelings. My mother did her best with what she had, and now I am doing my best to be a good parent, but I realize that even though I am there for her and I listen, there are no guarantees that what I am giving my daughter is exactly what she needs.

One of the most important things I try to teach Zoë is that it is OK to have your feelings, all of them; you just have to learn how to express them in a healthy way. Sometimes she is sent to her room to have those feelings. I don't know if my daughter will develop an unhealthy relationship with food, but I do know that today she sees both her parents eating healthy and exercising regularly. And whenever there is a house full of her friends, which is often, I can be counted on to bake, in Zoë's words, "the world's best cookies." Because today a cookie is simply a cookie and not a weapon I will use to punish myself later. For me, that is a sweet sign of how far I have come.

My friendships are amazing, most having survived my eating disorder. For my thirtieth birthday I had thirty of my closest girlfriends celebrate with me. Looking around the restaurant table, I realized I had gone through so many different experiences with these woman and they all meant so much to me. For a moment I stopped thinking about all those years I had fought any of my friends getting close enough to reveal my secrets. Now I celebrate them forming their own friendships separate from me because I have nothing to hide. My friends and I are loving and committed to each other.

I was married and together with my ex-husband for almost nine years. To be in any intimate relationship that long is a testament to all those years of working on myself. I've heard it said that you need to become the person you are seeking in a relationship. And while our marriage ended badly, making me doubt myself and lose self-esteem, I eventually recovered myself with the help of my spiritual beliefs, friends, and family. I learned so much about love and intimacy from my first husband, something I will always be grateful to him for.

I recently married again and moved from the place I had called home for eight years, the longest I have ever lived in one location. It was the first time Zoë had ever moved in her life. It is important to me to keep her life stable and consistent. She was able to stay in the same school and keep all her friends. I have a safe, secure marriage where I feel a love and acceptance that I had never experienced in my life. My husband and I truly know each other well, and it is because of that sense of safety, along with his support, that I was able to write this book. Mike is smart, kind, loving, romantic, funny, and supportive. He is also a WASP-y Republican who knows too much for his own good, which is bound to become the subject of another book one day. I recently told a friend that if I had to journey my entire life through tremendous obstacles both externally and internally in order to get to the life I live today, then it was well worth it.

Today I support myself as a writer. I am also a full-time mom, and stepmother to two amazing, creative girls, Kate and Alice, who I love more every day. My body is no longer my focus. I eat right, and that can include meat, sugar, dessert, and most things I want. I do yoga and run, usually three to five times a week, mostly for my peace of mind. All in all my life is far from perfect, but I am so grateful that it is mine.

Last year my mother moved to California, after having lived in Atlanta for the past ten years, unprepared but excited for this next step on her journey. It had been almost thirty years since we'd lived in the same city and had the opportunity to be together regularly. My husband remarked that my mother is warm, loving, and wise—nothing like the cold, distant version from my childhood that I had described. And she's not. "People are allowed to grow," my mother told me one day when I talked about the past. And she has. She discovered that she has a sensory disorder, which is why she couldn't stand sharp child-hood noises, but she has also learned a little more patience. At moments my mother and I could not be any closer. We share an intimacy and openness and tell each other our dreams for both ourselves and for each other. At times I have the relationship with her I've always craved; but at other times our differences get in our way. My mother can't believe I'm a capitalist, while I still can't believe she accepts so little help so often.

She recently went back to Atlanta to finish her degree, but I look forward to next year when she'll return to live in Cali-fornia. This time she'll have a plan, and we'll both be better prepared for her arrival.

When I look back to the first time I entered a twelve-step program over twenty years ago, I am surprised at how much my life has grown and changed. I actually have a life now. Occa-sionally I attend meetings to check in, to listen, and to be of support to those who still suffer. Today there are usually half a dozen black girls in the room, from all backgrounds. That's more than when I started, which is a sign of how far we've come that we are now seeking outside help without worrying about the stigma.

But the biggest change in my life is that even though I have made so many mistakes—big ones, huge ones, painful ones—I have taken responsibility. I have not used my mistakes and bad choices to make me believe that I am unworthy. I am human, and I accept that I am not perfect. But I no longer want to be. Nor is perfection a yardstick I use to measure myself or oth-ers. What I would like is to be a little better every day. To love myself, my family, and my friends a little better every chance that I get. I am amazed that I have lived through the hell of my eating disorder and that I not only talk about it but I no longer feel ashamed or traumatized by it. Hello, my name is Stephanie; I am anorexic, bulimic, a compulsive overeater, but I am also a mother, daughter, wife, friend, and writer, and I am grateful to be here today.

Acknowledgments

Thank you to my agent, Jennifer de la Fuente, who believed in this book from the very beginning and always knew we would publish it, and to Steven Malk, for sending my work to Jennifer and starting the process.

I am grateful to my editor at Chicago Review Press, Susan Betz, for bringing her insights as both a woman and a mother and for making this a painless experience. Thanks, Sue, for championing this book and for keeping me focused in the right direction. And thanks to my project editor, Lisa Reardon, for cleaning up my mess.

Mike, my husband: without your constant support, humor, and nurturing, I would not have had the strength to tell my truth.

Thanks to all the people who knowingly and unknowingly helped me through my eating disorder and recovery: Camilla, Cynthia, Kate, Pilar, Rae, Tiffany, the entire Agape family, especially Akili, Laterri, and mother Alice; John Barnes, Rev. Michael Beckwith, Terrah Bennett-Smith, Vondie Curtis-Hall, Meri Danquah, Juli Donald, Raye Dowell, Will

Flaherty, Annette Gartrell, Shelley Gerrard, Natalie Gluck, Hannes Jaenicke, Renee Jones, Jeff Joseph, Kasi Lemmons, Regina McLeod, Aireka Muse, Robi Reed, Salli Richardson-Whitfield, Elizabeth "Lisa" Sanchez, and Jessica Sharzer.

Thanks again to my sister Renee, who read the first draft of this book and added her memories, and to my brother Jasen, the one great thing my father has ever given to me. Thanks to my aunt Gerda Govine-Ituarte for always giving me a home and a strong sounding board, my cousin Jennifer, who read the first draft in one sitting and shared her memories, and Greg and Aunt Ethellee for making Virginia feel like home. And to Felicia, who shared all my childhood moments and made the good ones great and the bad ones better.

When I told my mother I needed to write this book, her response was, "Stephanie, tell your story, because after all, you lived it." I can't thank her enough for that, and for always telling me how proud she is with the life I have made for myself. Maybe now it's time to tell your story, Mom. And to all the members of my family whose names I didn't mention, you all gave me so many memories, many which were hilarious and loving.

Jeanne Williams, thanks for your daily insights and for always supporting me and keeping me laughing, but mostly for teaching me that's it not the hand we're dealt in life that defines us but instead how we choose to play that hand.

Thanks to Beebe Smith-Johnson for being a great big sister, to Helie Lee for showing me the discipline it takes to achieve my dream of becoming a writer, one word at a time, and to Treva Etienne, who was the first person to read a very rough first hundred pages and demanded I keep going. I'm not sure I would have been bold enough without your support.

To my other early readers, Jeanne, Juli, Kate, Jessica, and Camilla, I appreciate your reading through the bad grammar.

My heartfelt gratitude to my sister-girlfriends past and present, because I wouldn't be here today without your support, and to Roger Erickson, the world's best celebrity (and, clearly, noncelebrity) photographer and extra husband.

To my ex-husband, Arrisen Towner, thanks for being a loving and committed father and supportive coparent, coming through whenever I needed to write, and always agreeing that Zoë comes first. And thanks to my bonus daughters, Kate and Alice, for always keeping things exciting, interesting, and comical.

To the employees at my favorite writing spots, Starbucks on Larchmont, Insomnia on Beverly, and Solar Cahuenga, thanks for keeping me fed and caffeinated.

All the other people who warrant an acknowledgment for helping to grow me up are too numerous to mention. But please know that I could not have survived my addiction or recovery without you.